A Love Letter to Twentysomethings Everywhere

A Love Letter to Twentysomethings Everywhere

Yes, You *Can* Adult

Paul Shotsberger

Foreword by Hannah Selden

RESOURCE *Publications* • Eugene, Oregon

A LOVE LETTER TO TWENTYSOMETHINGS EVERYWHERE
Yes, You *Can* Adult

Copyright © 2021 Paul Shotsberger. All rights reserved. Except for brief quotations in critical publications or reviews, no part of this book may be reproduced in any manner without prior written permission from the publisher. Write: Permissions, Wipf and Stock Publishers, 199 W. 8th Ave., Suite 3, Eugene, OR 97401.

Resource Publications
An Imprint of Wipf and Stock Publishers
199 W. 8th Ave., Suite 3
Eugene, OR 97401

www.wipfandstock.com

PAPERBACK ISBN: 978-1-6667-1967-3
HARDCOVER ISBN: 978-1-6667-1968-0
EBOOK ISBN: 978-1-6667-1969-7

11/10/21

Unless otherwise noted, Scripture references are from Holy Bible, New Living Translation, copyright © 1996, 2004, 2015 by Tyndale House Foundation. Used by permission of Tyndale House Publishers, Inc., Carol Stream, Illinois 60188. All rights reserved.

Some additional Scripture references, as noted, are from The Message. Copyright © 1993, 1994, 1995, 1996, 2000, 2001, 2002. Used by permission of NavPress Publishing Group.

The Dream. Words and Music by Graeme Edge. Copyright © 1969 Gymhouse Ltd. Copyright renewed. All rights administered by Sony Music Publishing LLC, 424 Church Street, Suite 1200, Nashville, TN 37219. International copyright secured. All rights reserved. *Reprinted by permission of Hal Leonard LLC.*

To Lori Hatcher, the editor's editor. Thank you for opening my eyes to the possibilities within this book.

Contents

Foreword by Hannah Selden | ix
Acknowledgement | xiii
Introduction | xv

1 Promises and Growing Up | 1
2 Why Should I Be Afraid? | 9
3 A Hope and a Future | 17
4 Need for Healing | 23
5 Unexpected Miracles | 33
6 Growing Up Together | 42
7 Protection and Provision | 50
8 You're Never Too Young or Too Old | 59
9 Responding to God's Voice | 70

Conclusion | 76
Bibliography | 79

Foreword

WHEN I READ THE first few chapters of the manuscript of this book, I was sitting in a tree house after a tearful conversation with God. I had spent the previous hour stomping through a forest and telling him how much I resented and was exhausted by grief, how afraid I was looking toward the future, and how desperately I hoped that, amidst my suffering, I was still honoring him. I would graduate from college in just over four weeks, and, as far as I could tell, this transition would cost me everything.

What was I supposed to look forward to if not graduation? Shouldn't such a big step toward adulthood be exciting? Shouldn't I be proud of what I've done? All my life, I'd been told that life starts after school. But I saw no hope for the future. I knew my tomorrow wasn't promised but, honestly, I didn't want a tomorrow to prepare for anyway. I was being told that I had to grow up now and enter the big world, but everything within me revolted at that.

Paul witnessed this firsthand during my final semester. We had begun to meet for coffee every two weeks, with the intent of talking about the things I'd been writing. But my angst regarding that season of my life would seep into the conversation and became a topic of discussion. It was no coincidence that he was in my life during that time because I'm pretty sure Paul's calling is sitting with college students in turmoil and bringing God's peace. The

Foreword

Lord knew what I needed, and I found myself walking away from those sacred meetings not simply knowing, but also believing that someone like me could do it (whatever "it" happened to be).

He would tell stories about how he made mistakes, bumbled around, and felt out of control and confused, as I often do. But whenever he'd speak of great pain, confusion, perseverance, grief, or foolishness, he would smile with a confidence and courage that was both baffling and inspiring. I saw that he did not remember these things with regret but with peace. It took me too long to realize why. It's because he knows something that I didn't, learned something that we, as twentysomethings, forget. He did his best, and God did the rest. It had been that simple, that messy, and that beautiful.

As it turns out, Paul had been writing a book (spoiler alert: it's this book) on exactly that idea. As I read the first few chapters sitting in that tree house, I learned that my responsibility in all of this is not to do everything right. (Praise the Lord.) I wasn't expected to grow up with ease and poise. (Praise the LORD!!!) What God expected of me was something else: patience while waiting, faithfulness against all odds, and obedience even when I don't understand. He wants people who will trust through tears, struggle for what is right, and be okay with the awkward dance of being a messy human who loves and seeks to please a sweet and holy God.

I've always been good at crying and fighting and laughing, I thought, *so maybe I'm not as ill-equipped for growing up as I thought I was.* Maybe what I have to offer is exactly what God wants of me. Maybe my stumbling forward, putting one foot in front of the other, brings him as much glory as sprinting in perfect stride. Maybe the thing I've hated most about facing the journey before me is the very thing he rejoices in redeeming—my weakness.

All my life, I'd been told that freedom, independence, and purpose would lie on the other side of this challenge. But what I found in these pages is that that's not what "growing up" means or requires. Adulting is not a one-and-done act and it's not conquering giants and emerging unscathed. Rather, it is, again and again, taking God's promises in an open hand and surrendering to be an

Foreword

active participant in their realization. Woven into every story that Paul shares is his humanness and God's bowling bumpers of grace. It turns out that we need both of these things for a life of faith, and the real blessing is that we lack neither of them. I hope that this book brings you the same joy it brought me as you are reminded that God intentionally invites our messy selves into his story and is brought glory when they meet.

Hannah Selden
Class of 2021
Southern Wesleyan University

Acknowledgement

THIS BOOK IS WRITTEN from my memories of conversations with the people who have influenced my life. I pray that they will be useful in shaping the next generation.

Introduction

I'M IN MY SIXTIES in my body but twenty-five in my mind. Instead of me passing through generations as I get older, generations pass through me. Most people don't know anything about this strange phenomenon, but I've decided to let the current generation of twentysomethings in on my secret: I'm you, just with a bit more experience.

I was prompted to write because of a book by Ben Sasse that laments the hesitance of many young people to grow up and do adult things.[1] There are a scary number of books out now with the word "adulting" in the title; a new podcast is called "We Can't Adult." Many in their twenties don't want the pain or inconvenience of growing up and can't see the ultimate benefit.

You are my people. I'm a professor of undergraduate students and I attend a church populated by twentysomethings, so I spend at least six days a week with college and post-college age folk. Since in my mind I'm still in my twenties, I'm obviously in my element. But I've been through some stuff and have had days of growing up, so I wanted to share some of those stories. As Parker Palmer observes, "... many young people today journey in the dark, as the

---

1. Sasse, *The Vanishing American Adult*.

Introduction

young always have, and we elders do them a disservice when we withhold the shadowy parts of our lives."[2]

I want to help my students and friends understand where hope comes from for growing up. I'm concerned for you, those at the tail end of the Millennials and the beginning of Gen Z (born after 1996). I started teaching high school when I was twenty-five, and those were some of the most enjoyable years of my life. I was already married, my wife and I worked at the same school, and we thoroughly enjoyed our time together. These days, I hear post-college friends wishing their way through their twenties, hoping for better days. Relationships are a burden, work is a burden, finances are a burden—everything is a burden. The thought seems to be that if they can just get to their thirties, they'll have everything figured out and can finally feel like successful adults. But that's an illusion, as anyone who is in or has already passed through their thirties knows. We don't grow up because we hit some chronological age; we grow up when we decide to live, when we reach out and grasp hope by the tail and allow it to pull us into the future.

Let me return to Ben Sasse and his lament over the college and post-college hesitance or even refusal to do adult things. Here is his solution to the problem: hard work, travel, building a personal library, and nurturing physical health. There you have it, easy peasy. That might work for an older generation, but not the twentysomethings I love so much. Though Sasse and others (many others) are quick to criticize the way this generation was raised—the coddling, the hovering parents, the protection from the big, bad world—that's not what I choose to focus on in this book. That's because I know too much.

You are my students, but you are also my friends, and I see your struggles up close. I also remember the criticisms leveled at my generation, the Boomers, and the lashing our parents took for exactly the same reasons parents today are being taken to task. If someone had come up with the term "snowflake" back when Boomers were twentysomethings, we could have easily been given the same label. Yet, I suppose my generation turned out okay

---

2. Palmer, *Let Your Life Speak*, 18.

Introduction

because now we're running the world. As I tell my teacher candidates, if you stick around long enough, you'll wind up in charge. Assuredly, that will eventually happen for today's college and post-college crowd.

My concern isn't so much for the product as it is the process. What about right now? Gen Z is the most educated, diverse, and culturally aware generation in history.[3] You are also anxious people, and that anxiety has mostly to do with the future. At a relatively young age, many of you are on an array of prescription drugs and have weekly sessions with a psychiatrist or psychologist. I'm not downplaying the need for any of these things. I mean, just consider what you've already collectively experienced: 9/11, the Great Recession, myriad mass shootings, including school shootings, racial and political upheaval, and, of course, a worldwide pandemic.

Because of these collective experiences, as well as individual traumas, twentysomethings aren't waiting for a mid-life crisis as the Boomers did; many are fully engaged in what is known as a "quarter-life crisis." Why? There are many theories, but the clinical psychologist who originated the term, Alex Fowke says, "This can stem from a period of life following the major changes of adolescence, when a person doubts their own lives and faces the extent of the stresses associated with becoming an adult."[4] Bingo.

A recent informal survey completed at my university asked students of a particular major a few pointed questions. In return, the professor conducting the survey received some whiplash-inducing responses: 20% admitted to physically self-harming themselves, 35% had experienced suicidal ideation, and 80% revealed being "absolutely overwhelmed." This represents only one major on campus, but I believe the responses reflect and even underestimate the situation among undergraduates today. There seems to be neither support nor payoff for growing up.

A friend recently graduated from college and found a solid job with good pay and career potential. Personality conflicts soon

---

3. Parker & Igielnik, *On the Cusp of Adulthood*.
4. Fitzmaurice, "Quarter-Life Crisis," para. 6.

Introduction

emerged between her and her supervisor. Within four months of starting, she was seeking other work.

"Give it a year," I said, "It doesn't look good on your resume to jump around from job to job."

"I can't imagine working here another *week*," she said.

A popular term in educational research has emerged these days. We call it "grit"—perseverance and passion for long-term goals.[5] The good news is that grit can be taught; the bad news is that research isn't finding much evidence for it in the schools and colleges Gen Z attend.

I don't intend to criticize these tendencies because I understand where they come from. I also understand *who* they come from. Instead of offering criticism, I'd like to offer hope. Unlike Sasse's approach, which treats the symptoms but does not address the underlying human condition, I want to suggest a biblically sound solution.

Society has failed to take care of you. Because today's homes and families are broken, young people are unable to experience the stability they did even a few decades ago. As an educator, I'm also convinced schools are broken. If it's true, as Nel Noddings maintains, that "the main purposes of education are to help students find out what they are good at, what they would like to do with their lives, and how to live responsible and fulfilling lives,"[6] we have a problem. Today's education system, at all levels, is more concerned with test scores and performance than with preparing students to be functioning adults in society.

So who has your best interest at heart? It should be the church, but the problems and issues of twentysomethings are as prevalent inside the church as outside. In fact, Millennials and Gen Z are convinced the church has little to offer. Even if you call yourself a Christian, likely you don't attend any kind of formal worship except perhaps online. In a world of broken promises, the church is just one more—another source of condemnation, another dismissive voice telling you to just grow up.

---

5. Duckworth, *Grit*.
6. Noddings, *Philosophy of Education*, 66.

Introduction

I don't know about you, but I seem to have a constant need for the hope that promises offer us. I'm grateful to God to have had those kinds of promises in my life. I've written them down because they might be some encouragement to others, especially those readers who are waiting for a promise to be fulfilled. Promises may be for the short term, to ease some pain or fear, or for eternity, to finally "... have slipped the surly bonds of earth ... and touched the face of God."[7] Promises from God come in all shapes and sizes, through Scripture but also through circumstances in our lives. The most powerful promises are those made to us when we're at the end of our rope, when we understand there's nothing we can do to help ourselves. Then promises become our ally in the fight for resolution and satisfaction, and we cling to them for all they're worth. God delights in that kind of tenacity because it reflects the relentless love he has for us.

Early on, the kinds of promises I clung to involved justice in the face of bullying. As I got older, they had more to do with relationships, possessions, and the need for healing. I now have the satisfaction of looking back on my life knowing that the promises of God have all been realized save one, the promise of eternity. The most significant promises are those that have taken the longest to accomplish. When we're in the circumstances, it can seem like the wait for fulfillment is endless. Now, those are the very promises that mean the most to me. I hope you can see yourself in the stories I depict, and I hope you derive some encouragement not only that God keeps his promises, but also the vast array of ways our creative God accomplishes those promises.

I want to start this investigation with the Bible. I know that your experience with Scripture might be similar to that of Rachel Held Evans: "The Bible of my twenties served only as a stumbling block, a massive obstacle between me and the God I thought I knew."[8] But let me assure you that Scripture is a deep well of wisdom that we can draw from to answer many of life's most challenging questions. Do we have scriptural models for growing up? What

---

7. Magee, "High Flight."
8. Evans, *Inspired*, xvii.

Introduction

do those models have to do with God's promises? And what does all of that have to do with a generation that today is trying to claw its way up a mountain full of obstacles to gain some perspective on their lives and hope for their future? The answer is, believe it or not, everything.

Once we establish a biblical foundation for promises and growing up, then we'll move on to some personal stories I'll share with you about my own days of growing up, with all the associated stumbling and joy and terror along the way. I will conclude with a chapter on hearing and responding to God's voice. If promises are the stuff of growing up, then it's important that we're in a good place to receive those promises. So, let's get started.

1

Promises and Growing Up

I WANT TO MAKE the biblical connection between promises and growing up. Honestly, I hadn't fully considered the connection until I started writing my own stories as part of this book. But as they say, once I saw the connection, I couldn't unsee it. Though there are myriad promises of God I could point to, I'll narrow the focus to just two examples, one from each of the Old and New Testaments.

In the Old Testament, the inescapable promise that pervades almost every book is the land promised by God to the Jewish people, the land of Israel. This land of promise was the ultimate reason the Israelites left Egypt—it was the destination of their forty-year odyssey in the wilderness. Yet, by the time the Jewish people left Egypt, the original promise of land was already hundreds of years old. When Abram was given his missionary commission, he wasn't told simply to go. Gen 12:1 clarifies that God had a particular destination in mind: "The Lord had said to Abram, 'Leave your native country, your relatives, and your father's family, and go to the land that I will show you.'" Abram was promised that if he left home and family, God would move him to a new land. This promise was passed down from Abram as Abraham to his son Isaac to Isaac's son Jacob, and by extension, Jacob's son Joseph. When Joseph was near death in Egypt, he made the people take an oath that their

A Love Letter to Twentysomethings Everywhere

progeny would carry his bones into the Promised Land and give him a proper burial in that place.

So, the Israelites carried the promise of generations on their shoulders as they exited Egypt. And this is where we come to the connection between the promises of God and growing up. Can God keep his own promises? Yes, of course. But so often, for reasons that are beyond our comprehension, he hinges the fulfillment of his promises on the decisions of his followers, and those decisions have everything to do with growing up. If all God cared about was obedience, then he would give responsibility for fulfillment of promises to the angels. But he doesn't do that. Instead, he throws down the gauntlet of belief and obedience in front of his people and almost dares them to pick it up.

For the Promised Land, this challenge took the form of Moses commissioning spies to go into the territory, scope it out, and return with a report (Num 13). In fairness, the spies were faithful witnesses of what they saw. The land was bountiful, just as the people had hoped. Yet, there was a problem. It was also inhabited by super-sized people who lived in heavily fortified cities. Ten of the spies concluded their report by saying the Israelites were outmanned and outgunned, and the better part of valor was not to enter the Promised Land at all.

Only two spies, Caleb and Joshua, disagreed. You might be familiar with the rest of the story: An entire generation of Israelites died in the wilderness, and it was the next generation that finally entered the land, led at the front by Caleb and Joshua. Could God have required the older generation to enter the land anyway, despite the majority report from the spies? Yes, but that's not how God operates, it seems. He is as concerned about spiritual and emotional growth as he is about physical growth, and even if the older generation could enter the land, they would not have taken possession of it.

So, when exactly did God's people grow up in this Old Testament story? My opinion is that it happened on the day they crossed the Jordan River, before they'd fought their first battle. And as it often happens, their leader had to grow up first. It would not be

Promises and Growing Up

like it was for Moses and the people crossing the Red Sea, when the water opened up and they crossed on dry land. No, this time Joshua and the people (technically, the priests carrying the Ark of the Covenant) would have to step into the water before the parting took place. As I'll attempt to convey in the coming chapters, this is an uneasy place to find ourselves. All we have to go on is a promise. Did we hear God correctly? Did we make it all up? What if I step out in faith, nothing happens, and I look like a fool? Surely, this was on Joshua's mind, and that's why God spends an extended time encouraging him, over and over, to be courageous. First, he metaphorically slaps Joshua in the face with the reality, "Moses my servant is dead" (Jos 1:2), but then urges Joshua, "I will not fail you or abandon you. Be strong and courageous . . . Be strong and very courageous . . . be strong and courageous!" (Josh 1: 5, 6, 7, 9).

But what does courage really look like? It's rarely heroic. As is so often the case with God, what he desires from us is simply to put one foot in front of the other. It's then that God acts to keep his promise in a way that denies us the ability to believe it was of our own doing. One might think that we grow up because of seeing God's faithfulness, but it's also true that first we grow up, and then the promise is fulfilled. We have a part to play in the drama, despite the omnipotence of our good God. He desires partners, not minions, ". . . to do what is right, to love mercy, and to walk humbly with your God" (Mic 6:8)—that is a heart with whom God can co-labor.

In the New Testament, the greatest promise was given by Jesus to his followers at the Last Supper: "And I will ask the Father, and he will give you another Advocate, who will never leave you. He is the Holy Spirit, who leads into all truth . . ." (John 14:16–17). Why do I consider this to be the greatest promise in the New Testament? It's not only because the gift of the Holy Spirit is so inextricably tied up with the 2,000-year history of the church. It's also because that promise is the foundation of Jesus' statement that follows in John 14:18: "No, I will not abandon you as orphans—I will come to you." This isn't a reference to his second coming, since he hadn't left them yet. Jesus was readying himself for death by

A Love Letter to Twentysomethings Everywhere

crucifixion, then resurrection and ascension back to the Father. He created us, he sustains us, and he knows us. That means he knows our deep-seated fears over the possibility of abandonment. We all have an orphan spirit shivering within us, bracing itself for the inevitability of loneliness and loss. Our sinful nature wars against God's promise of companionship and advocacy. So the Apostle Paul says in his letter to the Romans that there are only two possibilities for the direction of our lives:

> Those who are dominated by the sinful nature think about sinful things, but those who are controlled by the Holy Spirit think about things that please the Spirit. So letting your sinful nature control your mind leads to death. But letting the Spirit control your mind leads to life and peace. For the sinful nature is always hostile to God. It never did obey God's laws, and it never will. That's why those who are still under the control of their sinful nature can never please God. (Rom 8:5–8)

The disciples had spent three years living 24/7 with Jesus, and as challenging as those years had been, they would be nothing compared to the days following the Last Supper. Jesus knew they would abandon him, but despite this, he promises not to desert them. The disciples surely must have felt abandoned after Jesus' death, but that feeling only lasted a few days. Then they had him back, learning from him like in the old days, but with new understanding. Surely he wouldn't leave them again, would he? But that was the plan. Yet, despite leaving earth for heaven, Jesus did not break his promise of not only walking alongside them but also living in them. Only ten days later, the Holy Spirit, otherwise known as the Spirit of Jesus (Phil 1:19), swept in among the followers of Christ and permanently changed the landscape of belief. Promise fulfilled. What about growing up? When did that happen for the disciples? What act of faith was required of them?

Certainly we can point to Pentecost and the transformation that took place among the disciples, especially Peter. They preached boldly and thousands came to salvation. However, the act of faith took place ten days earlier, at the ascension, when Jesus told his disciples to wait in Jerusalem "'... until the Father sends you the gift he promised, as I told you before. John baptized with water, but in just a few days you will be baptized with the Holy Spirit'" (Acts 1:4–5).

What had the disciples' experience been with the Holy Spirit up to that point, beyond the promise Jesus had given them? There is an intriguing scene that follows Jesus' resurrection. He commissions his followers to take the Gospel to the world, and "Then he breathed on them and said, 'Receive the Holy Spirit'" (John 20:22). This isn't a suggestion or a hope for the future; this is a command for that moment. I like to ask my students the question, "When were the disciples saved?" Usually they respond that his followers came to salvation by osmosis, during the three years with Jesus. But it doesn't really make sense that they could have been saved prior to the resurrection, when Jesus defeated death. My opinion is that salvation took place at this crucial scene following the resurrection when Jesus commanded them to receive the Holy Spirit. It's at this point that the disciples have everything they need to believe, to act in faith, and to mature into the leaders he needed for his fledgling church.

When Jesus then tells them to stay in Jerusalem and wait, there were none of the usual questions or complaints, the disciples' *modus operandi* for the previous three years. There was only obedience. Have you ever wondered why they had to wait for ten days? It seems excessive to be huddled in a room, no matter how large, with scores of people for over a week. I wonder, though, how many people they started with in order to finish with 120? Did everyone grow up? How many left before Pentecost? Also, I wonder what they were doing for all of those days. Was it just a marathon prayer session? We know they chose a replacement for Judas Iscariot, who had taken his own life, but what else? They might have had a lot of confessing to do with each other. Or maybe they just had a lot of growing up to do.

This group would be the nucleus of a worldwide movement that has spanned not only continents but also generations. It's a lot to ask of a bunch of fishermen and ne'er-do-wells. Yet, the 120 believed that whatever this baptism was, it was both necessary and sufficient to get the job done, and it was therefore worth the wait. It's important to note that in order for the Israelites to realize the fulfillment of their land of promise they had to act, to step into the Jordan River; for the disciples to see the fulfillment of their promised baptism, they had to wait, to not act. Had the Israelites not acted, they would have been disobedient; had the disciples acted, they would have been disobedient. As I've discovered in my own life, we grow up in many ways and on many days.

So, now we have at least the beginnings of a biblical basis for growing up into the promises of God. But what about us? Are the promises God gives today in any way comparable to these monumental promises of Scripture? More to the point, does God still speak as he did to Abram and to the disciples? And how do we discern between God's voice and our own selfish desires? I can talk myself into all kinds of goals for my life and just slap a label on them, calling them God's promises. There is danger there, certainly. But there's a much greater danger in ignoring God's promises and living without faith. Just look at what happened to the generation of the exodus. The twelve spies saw giants and fortifications, and ten of them decided things didn't quite add up. If God calls, he also equips, right? In their minds they clearly weren't prepared to battle such overwhelming forces, so this wasn't their fight.

We make these kinds of decisions all the time in our lives. Today, there's an easy kind of Christianity that regards difficulties and challenges with suspicion. When we run up against roadblocks and detours, a voice in our mind whispers the question of Satan to Eve in the garden: Did God really say? Perhaps we heard wrong, or maybe we never heard God to begin with. How can we be sure? A couple of things leap to my mind. First, God's promises never disagree with Scripture and always ultimately glorify him. If we hear God's voice, we can validate that word through the Bible. Have you been called to stand for truth amid personal accusation? So was Joseph of the Old Testament. Are you suffering despite caring for others? That happened to Job. Is no one believing you, even though your intentions are pure? Consider the life of Jeremiah, the

Promises and Growing Up

weeping prophet. Are you asking yourself and God how long you have to wait for the fulfillment of a promise? That was John the Baptist's question as he languished in prison.

Second, what do these biblical characters have in common beyond just their trials? They were humble, and they were concerned less with their own comfort than with glorifying God. How can we be certain of having heard God's voice? We can humble ourselves enough to listen, but also we can and should test the word we hear. The Apostle Paul encourages us in 1 Thess 5:19–21, "Do not stifle the Holy Spirit. Do not scoff at prophecies, but test everything that is said. Hold on to what is good." Testing is the essence of discernment. Hesitation once we're certain of what God desires of us is potentially fatal, as with the Israelites in the wilderness. But hesitation in order to be certain of God's promise is essential. There are as many problems caused by a lack of discernment as a lack of faith. We can think of the disciples waiting ten days in Jerusalem prior to Pentecost as a kind of testing of Jesus' promise that they would be baptized by the Spirit. First they waited, then they acted, and they and the world were transformed.

Still, what if we find ourselves in the years between Joseph's dreams and their fulfillment, or the ten days between the ascension and Pentecost, or the Saturday between the crucifixion and the resurrection, when all we have is God's promise? I won't sugarcoat the truth—it's just hard. Recall, however, that these kinds of circumstances produced some of the most profound verses of Scripture. We have the words of Job during his suffering:

> And after my body has decayed,
>   yet in my body I will see God!
> I will see him for myself.
>   Yes, I will see him with my own eyes.
>   I am overwhelmed at the thought! (Job 19: 26–27)

Or Habakkuk's words in the midst of loss:

> Even though the fig trees have no blossoms,
>   and there are no grapes on the vines;
> even though the olive crop fails,
>   and the fields lie empty and barren;

> even though the flocks die in the fields,
>> and the cattle barns are empty,
> yet I will rejoice in the Lord!
>> I will be joyful in the God of my salvation! (Hab 3: 17–18)

Or remember Peter's response to Jesus' question about whether the twelve intended to desert him as so many other followers had: "Simon Peter replied, 'Lord, to whom would we go? You have the words that give eternal life'" (John 6:68). The dark days are when we have the chance to grow into spiritual adulthood, if only we'll stay the course with God. And when we grow up, we have a newer, richer narrative, one that is uniquely our own.

And that brings me to my own stories of growing up, which encompass the rest of the book. I hope you'll find them helpful and even inspirational. Truthfully, I'm still growing up, and I hope to be doing so until the day I pass on from this life. We all have a lot of maturing to do, and that's a hopeful thing, something to look forward to. Who knows? Maybe today is the day.

2

Why Should I Be Afraid?

PROMISES AND GROWING UP often emerge from the circumstances of our lives. I was physically bullied from the time I started school until the end of sophomore year in high school. I was meek and mild-mannered and not athletic, so I was an easy target. I'd put my faith in Jesus in third grade and was baptized the following year. At my Baptist church this was a milestone event and worthy of an entire class on the subject. During the class, the teacher gave us the opportunity to choose a verse that would be read immediately prior to each person's baptism. My choice was Ps 27:1:

> The Lord is my light and my salvation—
> so why should I be afraid?
> The Lord is my fortress, protecting me from danger,
> so why should I tremble?

Fear was my constant companion growing up. My baptism verse represented an understanding I had with God: He was promising to be my protection, and I would cling to that promise.

I refused to fight back against the bullies, with one exception: my friends being wronged. Then, for whatever reason, I was a whirlwind. I recall my friend being harassed by a couple of bullies on the playground. I was filled with indignation. I didn't care what happened to me; I only cared that my friend wouldn't have to face

A Love Letter to Twentysomethings Everywhere

the same torment as me. Running down the hill at full speed with my arms extended and locked in front of me, I hit one bully with the force of a freight train, knocking him over, and rescuing my friend. My boldness surprised all of us. Despite moments of bravery, when I was threatened, I just took the bullies' abuse.

As I passed from grade to grade, the bullies changed, but the torment, which was mostly verbal but also physical, continued. Two boys that hung out together in middle school, one the brains and the other the brawn, were a consistent source of irritation for me. They sat across from me in Spanish class, openly mocking me, at least until the teacher caught them up short and told them to get back to work. Freshman year in high school, I actually had to face off physically with brawn-boy. My father had been an athlete in high school and was a devout football fan, so I foolishly went out for the football team, despite my lack of height, weight or strength. One day at practice we had one-on-one hitting drills, where the defensive man would try to get past the offensive lineman. The coach assigned me to stop brawn-boy. There was no need for prophecy—everyone knew what would happen. He knocked me down over and over. The coach had no consoling words for me, but instead put his arm around my adversary and confided, "Your opponent isn't always going to be so easy." Lions 1, Christians 0. Blessedly, my family and I moved from New York to New Jersey immediately following freshman year.

God was gracious to give me next-door neighbors my age the summer before tenth grade, two girls who introduced me to other high school students even before the start of the school year. The older girl was part of a bike club, and so I convinced my parents to buy me a new bicycle so I could be part of the club (my three-speed Schwinn just wouldn't cut it). The bike I chose was a white Raleigh ten-speed that could absolutely fly. This was another source of freedom for me, the freedom to explore the area and get to know my new home. The great disappointment of that summer was the news that the girls would move to Los Angeles before the beginning of the school year. But by that time I had my territory

Why Should I Be Afraid?

and my people marked out, and I was as ready as I could be for the start of the year at a new school.

Yet, one thing that persisted from New York to New Jersey was bullying. Once again, two students chose me as a target, one a smaller, angry kid, and his friend, a much larger threat. The bullying from the smaller student ended in the middle of tenth grade when I suddenly shot up. I grew an inch just in December. But the bullying from the bigger kid persisted throughout that year. If you've watched the first *Back to the Future* movie and if you remember how Biff would appear out of nowhere to bully George McFly, you have an idea what my life was like in tenth grade. My bully purposely, and it seemed omnipresently, followed me around and made threats. I intentionally walked home a different way from school every day trying to avoid him, but to little avail.

I need to pause here and make a parenthetical remark for parents who might be reading this. It's important for you to know that in all the years this had been happening, I'd never told my family about any of the bullying that was going on in my life. We want our parents to be proud of us, and being the target of bullying brings only shame. Most kids hide that shame well—they leave it for the privacy of their bedroom, crying and fretting in the darkness. On the outside I was at peace; on the inside I was in turmoil, year after year. Parents need to ask their children pointed questions during their growing-up years. When my parents would ask, "How was school?" my response, every time, was "fine." I, like many children, wasn't much of a conversationalist. I needed, I wanted, for my parents to pry the lid off the jar of my life. Parents need to ask more specific but open-ended questions, like, "Tell me about your day," "Tell me about your friends," "Are you having trouble with anyone at school?" Just as many of us do, my parents assumed that if everything looked good on the outside, then everything was fine on the inside.

Therefore, my anger and frustration had nowhere to go, no way to be expressed—except to God. I'd grown up in the church and learned early on through the stories of the Bible that God's power was way beyond my own. If there was any good that came

A Love Letter to Twentysomethings Everywhere

out of being bullied, it was that God's promises became a solace for me. God had restored my life by moving my family from New York to New Jersey, and I became convinced that God did not want me to live in fear the rest of my high school years. So, I prayed the Lord would do something about my bully, anything, to relieve me of this burden. And yes, the words "Take him out" might have even crossed my remorseless lips. Though I had a very enjoyable year, when tenth grade ended I breathed a sigh of relief, knowing I didn't have to see the bully at all during the summer. (I feel sorry for kids these days who have no refuge in the summers because of cyberbullying.) I believed God would deliver me; I had hope of this despite not understanding how the deliverance would happen.

That is, of course, the power of God's promises. As much as we want desperately to be delivered from our negative circumstances, though it may sound strange, there's almost a Christmas Eve kind of anticipation of a promise being fulfilled. It was thrilling beyond words to know that my omniscient, omnipotent Father had a plan to keep his Ps 27:1 promise. Though I needed to be faithful to what God had called me to do, my worry and anxiety could dissolve into his hands.

Despite this assurance, as I prepared for eleventh grade, there was dread in my heart. Then I heard the almost unbelievable news: The bully's family had moved to another town, and most amazing of all, they'd opted to take him with them. Though in my prayers I probably had in mind something more like God carrying out a hit on the bully, the sheer creativity of having the family move away brought a smile to my face and a lightness to my heart. Our trials bring us more understanding of Scripture than any teaching. I knew exactly what the psalmist meant when he wrote:

> From my earliest youth my enemies have persecuted me,
>   but they have never defeated me.
> My back is covered with cuts,
>   as if a farmer had plowed long furrows.
> But the Lord is good;
>   he has cut me free from the ropes of the ungodly. (Ps 129:2–4)

Why Should I Be Afraid?

This meant, for the first time in my school career, I could live without a constant threat hanging over my head, and I made the most of it. Free of this burden, I could become the person who I longed to be, confident and unburdened. At least until I went to college.

That's because high school wasn't the last time I was bullied. Though I would eventually graduate from the University of North Carolina at Chapel Hill as a math education major, for the first two years I was a pure math major. One of the fundamental differences between the majors was the requirement for math majors to take four semesters of either French, German or Russian, because those are the languages in which most of the great mathematicians wrote. I'd taken years of Spanish in high school, but that wasn't an option, so I chose German because of my family's heritage.

I'd never been, and continue not to be, very good with languages. But German was a different, an even more imposing animal than Spanish. By third semester I was struggling more than usual, having to read and critique plays in German without a word of English being spoken. For reasons that only became clear later, there was a young man in that third semester who made it his mission in life to harass and belittle me any and every time I said anything wrong in class. And of course, he could do this because he was fantastic at German. This went on all semester. I'd stand in front of class stumbling and fumbling my way through some critique, and Ashley would just laugh all the way through it. I'd never experienced such personal opposition in my life. The physical bullying I'd endured in my school career had morphed somehow into psychological bullying, calling into question the one thing I had been confident in, which was academics. I'll also mention that this was a difficult semester relationship-wise, and so the classroom wasn't the only place there was conflict in my life.

Yet, because of my history with bullying and because God had come to my rescue so many times in the past, I had a deep assurance that somehow justice would be done. I'd found Isaiah's words to be true:

A Love Letter to Twentysomethings Everywhere

> Because the Sovereign Lord helps me,
> I will not be disgraced.
> Therefore, I have set my face like a stone,
> determined to do his will.
> And I know that I will not be put to shame. (Isa 50:7)

The trick, I had learned, was not to take matters into my own hands. Not that I waited patiently, mind you. I wasn't a child any longer; I was bigger and stronger than my tormentor and could probably take him down. As tempting as that was, and as impatient as I could be, I knew from experience that it was infinitely better for me to wait for God to keep his promise than to fulfill it myself.

Mercifully, the semester finally ended, and we headed off on Christmas break. Ah, relief. That would be a special break because I attended a missions conference called Urbana in Illinois. Living in New Jersey but attending college in North Carolina, I never had the chance to see my friends over a long holiday break. But this vacation would be different, as we had a large group going to Urbana from InterVarsity Christian Fellowship, and I was close friends with many of them.

Urbana was where I first caught the vision for missions, learning at the feet of giants like Elisabeth Elliot Leach and John R. W. Stott. One result of the conference was a conversation with a representative of The Evangelical Alliance Mission and finding out about an opportunity for ministry in Austria. It was a kind of consolation from God—the reason, I convinced myself, I had opted for four semesters of German. So, a short-term missions trip to Austria was planned for the following summer, between sophomore and junior years. That trip, experienced on the cusp of becoming a twentysomething, gave me a heart for Europe, which would find its fulfillment in my family's and my service in Ukraine some twenty years later. Perhaps an even more important outcome of the conference was the chance to reconcile with the friend I had so much conflict with during the semester. As is the custom at Urbana, we shared a New Year's Eve communion meal together (with 25,000 of our closest friends) and then embraced each other.

Why Should I Be Afraid?

That did a lot to settle my spirit and give me hope that the coming semester could be different.

When January arrived, it was time to return to campus for spring semester. My simple prayer had been, "God, if there's a way that Ashley could not be in my fourth semester German class that would be amazing." The chances of this, though, were slim because there just weren't that many sections of German IV being offered. Still, I was hopeful, witnessing especially the reconciliation with my friend over the break. It turned out that God had a different deliverance in mind for my situation with Ashley. Prior to the start of classes, a good friend found me and told me breathlessly, "You'll never believe what happened over the break. Ashley got saved!" What? My nemesis, my thorn in the side from German class? Hearing the news, I could relate to a man named Ananias in the Book of Acts, who was told by God to minister to Saul, the Christian hater. "'But Lord,' exclaimed Ananias, 'I've heard many people talk about the terrible things this man has done to the believers in Jerusalem!'" (Acts 9:13). Lord, you mean Ashley, the persecutor of Christians? How is this possible?

Fortunately, much as Barnabas had done for Saul, introducing him to a skeptical church in Jerusalem after his salvation, my friend the next day escorted Ashley to my door, and we all sat together and talked about his conversion experience. It was a very humbling conversation. Ashley recounted his sins of the previous semester in German class. He said exactly what I knew: He had made it his mission to make my life miserable precisely because I was a believer. But then he told us something I didn't know. At the same time he had been exasperating me with his derision, I'd apparently been wearing him down with my silence because I refused to respond negatively to him. In fact, he told me, every time he would make a cutting comment, I'd just smile back at him. And this was one of the things that had made him wonder whether the whole Christianity thing might not be real after all.

I could have just written Ashley off in the fall, or I could have dished back to him what he was giving me. However, there was something deeper going on, something unseen. God was actually

A Love Letter to Twentysomethings Everywhere

preparing the soil for the Kingdom, sowing seed that eventually produced fruit, despite the seemingly hard ground in which the seed had been planted. What do I mean by fruit? I mean the extravagant way God keeps his promises, beyond anything we could hope for or accomplish on our own. Shortly after I received the revelation of Ashley's conversion, I became president of a chapter of InterVarsity at Chapel Hill. The term of office lasted one year. The following year, when Ashley and I were juniors, he became my successor.

But God had personal blessings in mind for me, far beyond InterVarsity. In our senior year, after a not-great living experience I had in fall semester with a party-boy international student, Ashley and I roomed together in the spring, and this was one of the most enjoyable semesters I had in college. In May, shortly after graduation, I was engaged to be married to a wonderful girl you'll hear more about in the next chapter. When it came time for the wedding, there was only one choice for best man: my former opponent, now my best friend, Ashley. Who but God could accomplish the keeping of a promise like that? As Allender and Longman observe in their book *The Cry of the Soul*, "God loves irony because He is the master of surprise."[1]

---

1. Allender and Longman, *The Cry of the Soul*, 168.

3

A Hope and a Future

FULFILLED PROMISES IN OUR lives grant us an open door to grow up, but that end isn't assured and the process can take a long time. In *Moments that Matter*, I told the story of meeting my future wife and then about a year later coming to understand, while on an NROTC midshipman cruise, that I would marry her. When God graciously revealed that to me, I also clearly understood that I wasn't to tell her, that God would show her in his time. So began a journey for Susan and me that continues today, over forty years later.

When I returned from the cruise, I was a man on a mission. I might not be able to tell her, but I sure could show her. It's important to note that I'm two years older than my wife. When you're out of college that age difference isn't terribly important, but in college, the difference between a senior and a sophomore is a serious matter. From the senior's perspective, the sophomore can seem too young. But from the sophomore's vantage, there can be questions about the senior's intentions. That was certainly the case with Susan, who wondered what had gotten into me. I'd been friendly before, but now I was, well, hovering. I was also concocting any excuse I could for us to be together. In my eyes, it wasn't enough for us simply to be in a large or even small group together. We had to have time to ourselves, to get to know each other, and for her to

A Love Letter to Twentysomethings Everywhere

see my heart. But that precious time just wouldn't materialize, as hard as I tried to make it happen.

With her misgivings about my intentions, and with my inability to tell her what God had revealed to me, we were both fairly frustrated, and that frustration lasted for about two months. We were blessed to have a mutual friend who eventually would be the maid of honor at our wedding, who was willing to listen to our varying complaints. First, my future wife would confide that she didn't know what to make of me and that she was "this close" to telling me just to leave her alone. Then a few days later, I'd pour out my heart about the lack of response I was getting, asking what in the world I had to do to get this girl's attention. Impressively, our friend kept all these complaints and questions confidential and never divulged them to either of us.

Still, there was movement. Gradually, over weeks and months, my future wife's heart started to melt. I remember distinctly when winter turned to spring in our relationship. I was bold to suggest we have a day together, just the two of us. By this time I played guitar passably well, having picked it up about two years earlier. What could be better than time spent in the park serenading my love? And afterward, we could get some dinner together at the local pizza place. A perfect day. The time to pick her up for our adventure came, and inspiration hit me. I was a big Moody Blues fan in high school and had long ago memorized the lyrics from all their albums. That included the poems written by their drummer Graeme Edge, which I considered great art. So, I collected a handful of brightly colored fall leaves from the ground, knocked on her door, and with no introduction handed them to her and began reciting a poem called "The Dream":

> When the white eagle of the North
> Is flying overhead
> And the browns, reds and golds of autumn
> Lie in the gutter, dead
> Remember then, the summer birds
> With wings of fire flaying
> Come to witness spring's new hope

A Hope and a Future

> Born of leaves decaying.
> As new life will come from death
> Love will come at leisure
> Love of love, love of life
> And giving without measure
> Gives in return a wondrous yearn
> For promise almost seen
> Live hand-in-hand
> And together we'll stand
> On the threshold of a dream.

There, I had spoken the word "love." I didn't say I was in love or that we should be in love, just "love." But that was enough. She turned to look at her roommate, who was standing next to her with her mouth agape. And the most amazing thing happened: There was no puzzled look, no slamming the door in my face. My future wife turned back toward me and smiled a smile that told me there had been a breakthrough.

That day together was glorious, the weather beautiful, the pizza delicious. Much later, after we married, my wife told me that at the pizza restaurant she marveled at how much I used my hands to eat—even salad. If bread wasn't handy for a pusher, I just used my fingers to get the food on the fork. Apparently this was new to her. Yet, thank goodness, when love is budding these quirks are endearing rather than disgusting.

I tell couples I counsel that this is one secret of a happy marriage. When we meet and are getting to know each other, we're often drawn to each other's differences. Whether it's personality or giftedness, we see the other as completing us, and we very much value what that person brings to the relationship. Somehow, though, once married, those differences that were once valued become nothing more than annoyances. We think, if not saying out loud, "Why can't they be more like me?" A long-running joke is that men get married hoping women will never change, and women get married hoping men *will* change. I'm in favor of learning and growing, but not at the expense of who God has created us to be. I've learned a few manners during my forty-one years of marriage and now I use my hands to eat much less than I used to.

A Love Letter to Twentysomethings Everywhere

But, I also have the assurance that my wife would not want me to change my giftedness just to conform to her own personality. If you can find a spouse like that, you've found a priceless treasure.

Not long after that special day, Susan had her own revelation about our future together. It was the late 1970s and on Saturday evenings everyone but everyone on campus watched *Saturday Night Live*. In those days there was no option to watch it on a phone or on a computer with a Fire Stick—all of that was in the future. There was only the common room, watching with dozens of other students. But part of the appeal of the show was laughing along with others. My girlfriend (I could call her that now) had somehow never seen *SNL*. I, on the other hand, had a sister-in-law who worked as a page for NBC in New York City and who had secured a ticket a couple of years earlier for me to see a dress rehearsal of the show. Those were the days of Bill Murray, Dan Aykroyd, John Belushi, and the original crew, and I had the best time.

I wanted Susan to experience the show, so I came and got her from her room on the seventh floor, and we took to the stairs, running down to the TV room on the second floor. At some point I realized I had outdistanced her and so stopped on the landing, turned around, and extended my hand to her. She told me later that when she saw me with my hand outstretched, God spoke to her as he had to me and told her we would marry. It would still take a few weeks before words of love and commitment came out of either of our mouths, but from that point on I could tell from the look in her eyes that God had been faithful to keep his promise to me.

But getting married is merely an opportunity to grow up—it guarantees nothing. Just because we have a promise from God, and just because we experience the fulfillment of that promise, often in supernatural ways, that does not exempt us from difficulties directly related to the promise. My future wife and I were head-over-heels in love and could not wait to be married. We got engaged telling everyone we'd be married in two years, once Susan had graduated from college. As sensible as that sounded, once we were parted because of my work with the Navy, the separation was almost unbearable. She was in North Carolina and I was in Florida. Further, neither of us was enjoying life much, she in college and me in the Navy's nuclear power school. Both pursuits paled compared to the reality of being inseparably joined. So, our promise of a two-year wait, made mostly to console our parents, became an eight-month engagement; we married when I was twenty-two and Susan was twenty. I don't doubt God's timing in shortening the wait, but it had its consequences.

Almost immediately, we left for a temporary duty station at the Brooklyn Naval Shipyard in New York City. We rented the second floor of a three-story house sight unseen in a residential area of Coney Island, which was no small commute from my work. Though we had Manhattan at our beck and call, and though we spent many enjoyable weekends attending musicals and exploring the city, I was also on duty a lot, including every fourth weekend when I had to stay aboard ship overnight. Susan was isolated on Coney Island, surrounded by a foreign culture that included a heavily Hasidic Jewish population and battling the cockroaches that infested our kitchen. We adopted a cat for her, but it was small comfort.

Living was easier at my next duty station, Newport, Rhode Island, right in the middle of an America's Cup summer in 1980. But those good times lasted only four months, and then it was on to my permanent ship assignment in Norfolk, Virginia, and the two six-month deployments that would follow. As much as we reveled in being married, and were so very grateful to live together as best friends and lovers, it was still a hard life. I tell anyone considering joining the military to evaluate carefully the impact that experience might have on any serious relationship with a significant other.

My point is simply that after the promise of marriage was fulfilled, there was work to be done. God has his part, but we have ours, and sometimes it's not a part we would choose for ourselves. Yet, it's worth the work and the perseverance, and it is in fact how we grow up. Looking back on forty-one years of marriage, I know our relationship and each of us as individuals is stronger because of those times we simply had to endure. The Apostle Peter makes the connection between promises and endurance:

A Love Letter to Twentysomethings Everywhere

> In view of all this, make every effort to respond to God's promises. Supplement your faith with a generous provision of moral excellence, and moral excellence with knowledge, and knowledge with self-control, and self-control with patient endurance, and patient endurance with godliness, and godliness with brotherly affection, and brotherly affection with love for everyone. (2 Pet 1: 5–7)

Perseverance in promises makes a powerful difference in our lives, resulting not only in stronger relationships as I've illustrated, but godliness as well.

All of God's promises when fulfilled result in blessings for us, but more importantly, they should produce praise and glory for God through living out a godly life. I'm convinced this is a missing link for many Christians. We cling to the promises of God, we enjoy the fruit of a promise realized in our lives, but we fall short of God's expectations for worship. I'm as guilty of this as anyone. For some, this response is almost second nature, but I suspect that isn't the case for most of us, at least in the Western Church. We can feel, though we would hardly say, that we're owed God's blessing, and so we become blasé about the fulfillment of his promises.

Many through the centuries have wondered at the inclusion of the Book of Ecclesiastes in the biblical canon, with its somber message of "all is vanity." One thing it accomplishes, though, is providing us with a clear picture of what we're owed in this life. The short answer is, not much. There's a lot of hard work, too much injustice, and little of lasting value. But what's the Teacher's conclusion? ". . . Fear God and obey his commands, for this is everyone's duty" (Eccl 12:13). That the God of the universe not only thinks about us but also promises any good thing to us is remarkable. That God then brings a promise to pass is a grace beyond any expectation we could have for this life. What should our response be? The Christmas carol "O Holy Night" is one of my favorites. There's a phrase in it that gets me every time: "Fall on your knees." This shouldn't be our response only to the Christmas miracle; it should be the response to every kept promise of God throughout our entire lives. This is how we grow up, every day.

4

Need for Healing

IT'S DIFFICULT TO MATURE into responsible adulthood when we're not well. More often than not the connection between the promises of God and growing up is anything but a straight line—our emotional maladies can wrench that path into a spaghetti-twisted mess. Shortly after being released from prison for conviction on federal charges of mail and wire fraud and conspiring to defraud the public, Reverend Jim Bakker wrote, "I am convinced that many Christian people are forgiven of their sins, but they have never been healed of that sin's impact in their lives."[1] I couldn't agree more.

So many Christians today are among the walking wounded, unable to engage in the spiritual battle all around us because we're too weak emotionally and spiritually to even put on our armor. We were wounded as children or adolescents, by parents, siblings, bullies, and teachers, unbelievers and believers alike. Traumatic events opened doors for fear, and that fear has grown inside us for years, until now we're paralyzed. I'm someone who absorbs frustration and anger rather than reacts outwardly to it. I've already recounted the effect bullying had on me in my early years. Parallel to that were the expectations of my parents, especially my father.

Dad was bigger than life, an athlete in high school and college shaped by the Depression and his service in World War 2. By the

1. Bakker, *Refuge*, 140.

A Love Letter to Twentysomethings Everywhere

time I was in high school, my father had been with his company for over twenty years. He had climbed the ladder from salesperson to marketing director to executive vice president in charge of a U.S. operation that yearly amassed one billion dollars in sales back in the 1970s when a billion dollars was a lot of money. He was a titan of industry in every sense of the expression.

There was a lot to admire about my father, but also a lot to fear. He had all the answers to life's questions, and so his expectation for perfection was unrelenting. That expectation mixed with my fear of failure proved to be a toxic cocktail that would have me reeling into my mid-forties. For good or for ill, Dad was integral to my growing up; he was the rock I could hang onto when life became slippery, but he was also the rock that occasionally fell on me with disappointment and criticism. As with so many parent-child relationships, ours was a complicated existence.

My father fully expected me to make the military a career, just as he wished he had. In his fascinating analysis of father-son relationships, Fredrik Backman notes, "That's an impossible thing for sons to grasp, and a source of shame for fathers to have to admit: that we don't want our children to pursue their own dreams or walk in our footsteps. We want to walk in their footsteps while they pursue our dreams."[2] In Dad's mind, everything I accomplished or experienced while living at home—my performance at school, my hobby of building model ships and planes, our time visiting naval stations—should funnel me toward the Navy.

The day we were notified that I received an NROTC scholarship was one of the happiest for my father; my decision, at twenty-five, to leave the active duty Navy after only four years was one of his greatest disappointments. He enjoyed calling me Lieutenant Shotsberger, and he didn't value the teaching profession I chose over a naval career. It wasn't until I earned my PhD and my father could call me Doctor Shotsberger that I recovered his esteem.

The downside of me getting an NROTC scholarship and going to college, for my father, was that I was far from home and being exposed to new and different experiences. As a result, I was

---

2. Backman, *Anxious People*, 30.

Need for Healing

coming to new and different understandings. My parents made sure I had a sheltered childhood growing up. True, I had watched the Beatles perform on *The Ed Sullivan show*, but that was by accident because my family always watched that show on Sunday evenings. Yes, I saw the casualty figures coming out of Vietnam every night on the news, but those statistics were never connected to the question of an unjust war. After all, that might have discouraged me from a military career.

Over my time in college, I came to understand how ignorant I was of the world, and I was desperate to fill in the gaps. I was progressively focusing less on my major courses and more on electives, and as a result, my GPA was not particularly stellar. But my academic performance was more my father's concern than mine. In the spring of 1979, my last semester of college, I was delighted that there was a course being offered on post-World War 2 history, the centerpiece of which was the Vietnam War—its origins and its politics. The history was incredibly fresh—at that point, we were only six years removed from the U.S. withdrawal from the Vietnam conflict, and four years from the fall of Saigon.

In that course, at the age of twenty-one, I swam in a sea of knowledge that was revelatory for me: the history of the politics that drove America's entry into the war, all the protests and riots reflecting just how unpopular the Vietnam War had become, and society's derision of those who served once they returned from duty. How could I have lived through this time and known so little about it? Though the course was deeply meaningful to me, it resulted in a grade of C, and that meant that my GPA slipped below 3.0 just in time for graduation. My father and I were angry, but for very different reasons. He was livid about the grade; I was deeply resentful about the silence I had experienced growing up. I didn't confront him though; I just swallowed the anger, again. I was graduating college, going into the Navy, and soon to be married. I looked at all this as freedom, a welcome escape from my father's rule. Still, there was a sickness inside me crying out for healing.

༄ ༄

A Love Letter to Twentysomethings Everywhere

My father taught me a lot about life, but never more than through his death. Dad was intentional about whatever he did in life—everything was done for a purpose. He also never rang me on the phone just to chat. So when he called in the summer of 1992, I knew something was up.

My father said, "I have prostate cancer, and it's already out of the capsule."

I didn't even know what a prostate was.

"What does that mean?" I asked.

"It's in an advanced stage. It might be treatable, but nobody's sure."

"Is it something you could die from?"

"Yes, it's possible."

I was thirty-five years old and headed into the third year of my doctoral program.

My dad's focus was on my graduation, which he intended to see no matter what. It's remarkable the power the mind can exert over the body. Despite a debilitating condition, if we decide something in our lives still needs to be done, it will likely be accomplished before we're overcome. After three years in my program, I graduated from UNC Chapel Hill with my doctoral degree. Dad was smiling but he was also careful in his movements. By that time, I had convinced myself that he would beat the cancer. Mom and Dad had visited a clinic for specialized treatments, which seemed to be working. But then came the news the summer after my graduation that the cancer was spreading. He had achieved his goal of attending my commencement, and in short order, his health declined precipitously.

I graduated in May 1993, and by November of that year, my father was dead. I was a new professor in a new city with my wife of thirteen years and a four-year-old son. What did I know about life and a career and raising a family? Who would I go to with my questions?

Friends of my father were so kind in the years following his death. Our family traveled to Pennsylvania, where my father was from, and also to Maryland, where good friends lived. They would

Need for Healing

regale me with stories from the past, making sure I understood how special my father had been to them. One friend even told me that Dad had thought the sun rose and set on me, something that he had failed to communicate to me while he was alive. Their words were a kindness I could not repay, and they helped to ease the loss. But even with all of that support, I didn't know how I would carry on with my life.

A difficult thing about losing someone so influential in our lives is that we don't just lose them once. That's how the world imagines it, but it's not true. The world sees our loss taking place on a single day, and the funeral and the grief taking place on another day. But we lose these significant people over and over, day after day, sometimes for years. In one way, this is honoring to the person who died; we don't want them to be quickly forgotten, so at least initially the grief can feel appropriate and necessary. There's some undefinable crossroad, however, where we begin to drown in loss and sadness, and depression consumes our lives. Eventually a kind of *rigor mortis* sets in, and we realize that we have also died.

First Samuel 16:1 presents us with a similar situation. Saul had been anointed as king by Samuel, the prophet. After a hopeful beginning, Saul relied less on God and more on his own judgment, which was flawed. Ultimately, he disobeyed a direct command from God. Though Saul had been a frustration for Samuel, he continued to be an advocate of Saul's before God. Finally, God had had enough. And so we come to 1 Sam 16:1, the intersection of three lives: "Now the Lord said to Samuel, 'You have mourned long enough for Saul. I have rejected him as king of Israel, so fill your flask with olive oil and go to Bethlehem. Find a man named Jesse who lives there, for I have selected one of his sons to be my king.'" As harsh as it seems, God had to shake Samuel and tell him to get over Saul and get on with his mission, which was to anoint the new king of Israel, David. Sometimes when we're mired in grief and self-pity, God graciously gives us the promise that he has more for us to do, just as he did for Samuel. I couldn't have imagined the creative way God would make that promise to me.

A Love Letter to Twentysomethings Everywhere

For the next year and a half following Dad's funeral, I muddled my way through life, staying busy, hiding my loss in activity. In August 1995, there was a celebration of the fiftieth anniversary of VJ Day in Wilmington, NC, at the site of the USS North Carolina battleship memorial. My father had served on Tarawa Island in the Pacific war, and I wanted to represent him at the ceremony. Rather than having a typical wreath-laying at a cemetery, service members on board the battleship took turns throwing wreaths into the river, one for each branch of service, as a bugler played taps. Some World War 2 vintage bombers and fighters flew over the battleship, and the commemoration ended. The ceremony was heartfelt and very moving; my father would have enjoyed being there along with the many veterans in attendance.

Once home, I read in the newspaper that the aircraft used in the flyover would depart the Wilmington airport the next day at a particular time. Somehow I knew I had to be there—this, it turned out, was a day for promises. I settled onto a promontory overlooking the airport as the aircraft engines were turning up. One by one they took to the sky, first the fighters, then the bombers. The last to leave was the largest of the airplanes, a B-17 Flying Fortress, the aircraft most responsible for the Allied victory in Europe. It lumbered down the runway and lifted heavily into the air, its landing gear tucking into the tired body of the aircraft.

As the plane disappeared in the distance, I sensed I was watching the spirit of my father departing the earth. God spoke to my spirit as he had to Samuel: "This is the end; it's time to move on." Those planes represented my father's generation, the Greatest Generation, and now that generation was fading away. The strange thing was, unlike at the funeral, no tears came to my eyes. It was an end, but also a beginning, a new promise. There was only hope in my heart that God was back at the controls of my life, assuring me everything would be alright. The weight of the previous two years lifted from my shoulders—I could breathe again.

Need for Healing

Despite this newfound hope, as with a city shaken by an earthquake, there were aftershocks from my father's death that would ripple throughout the next seven years of my life. Dad's untimely end unleashed pent up anger in my life, not only because he was no longer around but also because I had swallowed so much negative emotion growing up. After my father was gone, that anger frothed up like a boiling pot of water, scalding my wife and son. The smallest thing could set me off, even something that should have been joyous.

I turned forty years old in 1997, and my wife had planned a special surprise celebration for that day. She had gone to great lengths to round up our closest friends and have them meet us at a restaurant on the waterway. A pontoon boat would take us on a brief excursion, and then we'd return to the restaurant for dinner. At that point, Susan and I had been married seventeen years and so she was confident that I would enjoy what she had planned. But there was a problem, or actually three: I don't like surprises, or crowds, or being the center of attention.

We rounded the corner of the restaurant and came face-to-face with a gaggle of our friends, all shouting "Happy Birthday!" My heart sank. Susan excitedly told me the plan for the evening and we promptly boarded the boat for the trip around the waterway. The celebration particularly energized my wife, and she flitted from one group of friends to the next, making sure everyone was having a good time. At one point, we passed by a boat being driven by John Boy Isley, a radio personality from the John Boy and Billy Big Show. Susan waved wildly to him as we passed by, shouting, "Hey John Boy, where's Billy?!" I melted into the boat deck, mortified. She was clearly having a much better time than I was, and I suspected that she had done all her planning based not on what I would enjoy, but what she found fun and exciting.

We returned to the restaurant and had what anyone else would consider a lovely meal, with our friends offering gifts for me to open. In my wife's thinking, everything had gone perfectly. My mind, however, clouded over in a seething rage. When we arrived back at home, I unloaded with both barrels: "How could

A Love Letter to Twentysomethings Everywhere

you humiliate me like that? What were you thinking?" Susan was stunned, unable to imagine how I wouldn't consider the evening a monumental success. Then, it was her turn to be hurt and angry. It was the worst fight we ever had as a married couple.

I had the promise from God that everything would be okay following my father's death, but the path from that promise to growing into mature, stable adulthood required emotional healing. As young children, we experience rejection by mother, father, sisters, brothers, friends, and teachers, sometimes in very traumatic and memorable ways. I have vivid memories of more than one time being seated behind a partition, placed there by the teacher I had for first and second grades, unable to see what was happening in the classroom but hearing everything. For some unknown reason the teacher rejected me, over and over, deciding to make me an example for my friends at school. But, I often also experienced rejection from my parents, especially my father, whose standard for me was perfection.

What does this kind of rejection result in? It causes us to feel in our emotions and believe in our minds that we're flawed, substandard, and not worthy of respect. When these feelings take up residence in our lives, they speak to us, causing us to think negatively about ourselves. Have you ever whispered to yourself, "You stupid idiot, now look what you've done. You always do things like that. How come everyone else can get it right, but you can't?" These kinds of thoughts eventually result in the belief that we'll never amount to anything, and for Christians, that we can't do anything significant for God. The Bible's promises are for someone else, someone respectable, not us. This line of thinking naturally leads to anger and frustration, and it's what I needed healing from.

As I shared in *Moments that Matter*, a retired pastor came to our church in 2001 to fill the pulpit until we could find a permanent replacement. God's timing was perfect because Dick Robinson's mission in life was ministering healing to broken people. His ministry had three parts to it: release of control to God, deliverance,

Need for Healing

and healing of memories. If you'd like to know more about these forms of healing, I encourage you to read Dick's book.[3]

For this book, I'll simply say that his ministry was transformational. It freed me from both the expectation for perfection (mine and others) and the crippling fear of failure. As at the Wilmington airport, when I watched the last of the World War 2 aircraft lift into the air, a burden was lifted. On that occasion, the relief was due to receiving the promise that everything would be okay after my father's death. This time, with my healing, I experienced the fulfillment of the promise, and it gave me not only hope for the future, but the reality of a new and healthier present.

As a postscript to this story, I want to express how important it is to be healed of the traumas in our lives as early as possible. The Boomers are renowned for our mid-life crises, which is why we buy bigger houses, drive faster cars (usually convertibles), and get divorced and remarried at a break-neck pace. Perhaps the greatest value of the quarter-life crises faced by twentysomethings these days is the early recognition of the need for healing. I never cease to be impressed with how self-aware my Millennial and Gen Z friends are, quickly recognizing a need in their life, wanting to better understand how God has gifted them, and being willing to follow God into the breach of calling and even spiritual warfare. These realizations would wait for me until I was in my forties. It was only then that I understood I had stage four spiritual cancer and the only effective cure was an aggressive and painful treatment by the Spiritual Surgeon.

My dear twentysomething friends, please don't wait as long as I did. It's not worth it. Be willing to admit your spiritual and emotional sickness to God and allow him gently to heal you. Let God help you identify the source of your pain. As Evans observes, "... there are demons in our stories that can only be cast out when we call them by name."[4] The longer you wait, the more painful the process. As with any physical malady, early detection and prevention is infinitely preferable to emergency surgery. Proverbs 3:5–8 is

3. Robinson, *More Than We Can Imagine*.
4. Evans, *Inspired*, 18.

A Love Letter to Twentysomethings Everywhere

a promise that, if taken to heart and pursued relentlessly, can lead us to complete healing and robust, stable adulthood:

> Trust in the Lord with all your heart;
> > do not depend on your own understanding.
>
> Seek his will in all you do,
> > and he will show you which path to take.
>
> Don't be impressed with your own wisdom.
> > Instead, fear the Lord and turn away from evil.
>
> Then you will have healing for your body
> > and strength for your bones.

Do this for yourself, your family, your work, your church, and your community. Do it for all of us.

5

Unexpected Miracles

Part of growing into adulthood is growing in faith, and many of those days of growing up for me have involved miracles of healing and of multiplication. All the miracles in my life have been unexpected. That speaks to our ever-surprising God, but also the microscopic size of my faith. Some have asked whether I have the gift of healing, because healings are part of my story. I tell people, "No, I've simply been in places where God has demonstrated his power." In fact, the first miracle I experienced wasn't one I'd even prayed for, though it spoke deeply to me about the Father's compassionate heart for his children.

When I left active military service in my twenties, I had severe issues with my back, likely because of the physical and emotional strains of shipboard life. Once I began teaching, it seemed like the smallest thing could put me out of commission. I was walking across the parking lot of our church and suddenly had to sneeze. When I did, my back seized up and I had to be helped to the car. That put me in bed for days. This, unfortunately, was normal, so normal that I soon was going to the chiropractor every week, sometimes two and three times a week.

This went on for years until finally it seemed my back was strengthening—my appointments were monthly, and I was sure that soon the chiropractor would release me from his care. Then,

A Love Letter to Twentysomethings Everywhere

the accident happened. A car pulled out in front of me at an intersection, and my little Toyota Corolla passed the impact from its front end directly to my neck and back. I immediately returned to multiple therapies a week and soon despaired of ever being free from debilitating back pain.

Therapies were annoying because it seemed when I was lying on my stomach, with the electrodes on my back that instead of the electrical pulses relaxing my back, they actually caused it to go into spasm. So, after many years of chiropractic appointments, it was my practice to flex my back during treatment to stay limber and have some kind of hope of getting up from the table under my own power. One time, though, I was exhausted and fell into a deep sleep on the table. Looking back now, I liken this to God causing Adam to slumber while removing his rib. I only awoke when the chiropractor's assistant started removing the leads from my back. I did not know how long I'd been sleeping, but it had to be about twenty minutes. I dreaded what was coming next.

I prepared to haul myself up from the table in stiffness and agony. Instead, easy as you please, I swung my legs around and sat up on the table, as if I was a young boy. "That's funny," I thought. I then hopped off the table and noticed there was no stiffness, that in fact my back was strangely flexible and pain free. I followed the assistant to the reception area, paid for the visit, and walked out of the office. I have not had the need for a chiropractor since that day. God had healed me in an instant, unexpectedly, and without a specific prayer being prayed other than a lament. He had shown mercy to me, but it felt like love, and it became a kind of promise for my life. God loved me enough to look down on my misery and have pity on me. That day, I grew up into a more spiritual adult because I accepted that I was worthy of a miracle from God. We all are.

But this was just the beginning of my experience with miracles. In the few years between my healing in the chiropractor's office and becoming a missionary to Ukraine, I was honored to be asked to lead a weekly healing service at my church. This was another place that my faith could mature, inspired by a handful of older women with the gift of faith who prayed for others. They fully believed God would heal everyone who asked for prayer, but they also had the tenacity to keep praying, week after week, when the healing wasn't immediately forthcoming. This impressed me, and gradually I learned to have the same faith, with the same wonderful results. This was a prelude for going overseas.

Following independence from the Soviet Union in 1991, Ukraine opened its doors to visitors from around the world, including evangelists. Those preachers, most with a charismatic bent, held large open-air gatherings where hundreds and thousands of Ukrainians came to faith, often because of the healing miracles they witnessed. This was the foundation of their belief in God. Therefore, miracles became an expectation, much as with the first century church in the Book of Acts. When Ukrainian believers had the opportunity to exercise their faith muscles, most were eager to join in, much like the older women I'd observed in the healing services.

Foreign visitors to the Ukrainian churches were often there for teaching and training, and the people of those churches lapped up the insights those pastors and others shared like the life-giving water it was. While we were living in Ukraine, a pastor in Virginia offered to bring with him some of his parishioners and conduct a healing workshop at one church associated with our institute. The workshop would take place over a week's time, and the general structure involved training during the day and hands-on experience in the evenings in the form of healing services held at the host church. Though I'd conducted healing services before, I had no formal training in prayer for healing, so I was excited about being part of the workshop.

There are many Christians who believe God causes sickness to test us or to mature us. This pastor made the point that sickness is a manifestation of our fallen world, of evil itself, and it's not from our good Father; in fact, it's something to be expunged. This follows the models of Jesus, who we're told healed everyone who came to him (Luke 6:19). When he encountered sickness, his heart was always to restore the person's health, not only physically

A Love Letter to Twentysomethings Everywhere

but also spiritually and emotionally. We say that God is the same yesterday, today, and forever, and so we can embrace the promise that healing is still God's heart for us.

The most important thing I learned that week was the concept of progressive healing. When we think of miracles, we imagine something instantaneous, much as I'd experienced with my back a few years earlier. But many times miracles, especially those that involve healing and, therefore, prayer for healing, come in waves. The example given to us during the workshop was Jesus praying for the healing of a blind man:

> When they arrived at Bethsaida, some people brought a blind man to Jesus, and they begged him to touch the man and heal him. Jesus took the blind man by the hand and led him out of the village. Then, spitting on the man's eyes, he laid his hands on him and asked, "Can you see anything now?" The man looked around. "Yes," he said, "I see people, but I can't see them very clearly. They look like trees walking around." Then Jesus placed his hands on the man's eyes again, and his eyes were opened. His sight was completely restored, and he could see everything clearly. (Mark 8: 22–25)

Whereas most of the healings of Jesus recorded for us in the gospels appeared to be instantaneous, in this case there was a definable progression and, in fact, a pattern that we could follow:

1. Pray for healing
2. Ask for a report
3. Continue praying
4. Ask for an update

We could continue this process until progress was evident. Even if healing wasn't complete, there was now a basis for the person being prayed for to believe that healing was on the way. The process seemed simple, but I and others attending the workshop had never encountered this method, and we were keen to try it out.

Unexpected Miracles

We didn't have long to wait. That evening the church hosting the workshop held a healing service outside the capital of Kyiv in a drafty auditorium with old wooden seats. The pastor who was leading the workshop preached on faith, and then those of us attending the workshop fanned out in pairs across the front of the church and waited to pray for people. It was at that moment that the reality of what we were doing hit me. The people lining up in front of us were expecting healing from our hands, right then. In the past, I'd seen times that those coming for prayer went away without healing and without hope, and I didn't want that to happen. I pleaded with God to let this experience be different, filled with miracles. A peace settled on me, and I sensed God assuring me that if I would just be faithful, he would take care of the rest. Some promises are for a lifetime, but some for only a moment; I leaned heavily on that promise that evening.

An older woman came up to us dressed in a heavy coat and headscarf, the typical garb of a grandmother, a *babushka* (pronounced BA-bushka, not ba-BU-shka as foreigners pronounce it). She told us she had been gradually losing her sight and now she couldn't read. "I just want to read my Bible," she said. I thought that was a reasonable request and certainly one God would honor. So we prayed, and after a few minutes we asked her if anything had changed. She said "No." But, of course, the actual test was her ability to see. So I asked for the Russian Bible of my prayer partner and translator. I looked at it and knew in that moment that God has a sense of humor because the Bible was a pocket version with tiny print. I murmured to myself, "Come on God, give me a break!" But I handed her the Bible anyway. She scanned the page and told us she could read "Gospel of John" in larger print at the top. We were all encouraged, so we kept on praying. After a few more minutes, we handed the Bible to her again and asked if she could read any more of the page. She read the text with ease. I'll admit to you I was shocked. It shouldn't have been surprising; it was exactly what we'd prayed for. But to see it in person, to witness the joy of the woman at her rediscovered sight—it was overwhelming.

A Love Letter to Twentysomethings Everywhere

But we weren't finished because there were many more waiting for prayer. I could share story after story, but I'll let one more suffice. A young woman came to us and said she had undergone surgery on one eye, and now for whatever reason the eye was dry. It couldn't produce its own tears. She was attractive, thirty-something, and vital. But there was also a sadness about her. She told us that not only did she have to put artificial tears into her eye every day, but there was almost constant pain. She wondered if God could heal her eye. Without saying anything, in my faithless way, I wondered the same thing. It was obvious, though, that this woman had a courageous faith. So we prayed. As we had been taught, after a few minutes we stopped and asked for a report. She told us she didn't feel any pain in the eye. We were ecstatic, and I'll confess that I believed that was all that would happen.

Yet, we followed the pattern and continued to pray. I had my hand on the side of her head, near the affected eye, and that area was getting hot to the touch. I'd experienced this before, and so for the first time it occurred to me that God might have more for her. We stopped praying and asked if anything was happening. Without a word, she took her little finger, put it up to her tear duct, and then held out her hand. There on the end of her finger was a drop of liquid, a tear formed naturally in her eye, just as we'd prayed. Her smile lit up the room. My prayer partner and I were stunned into silence, awed at both the power and the compassion of God to answer our prayers in such a wonderfully specific way. It's paradoxical how we can pray for something, and then when it happens we're surprised. My prayer partner and I floated out of the room that night. When we gave our report to the workshop the next day, there were cheers all around for God.

This wasn't the end of the surprises God had in store for me overseas. After serving in Ukraine, and once we returned to the States, the church we attended had a strong connection with a church in Nicaragua. We sent teams down yearly to Managua. Having been a missionary, the reports of those returning from these trips always energized me. They'd travel to the towns surrounding Managua, bringing with them donated items from our church: clothing, shoes, toys, and toiletries. During one team's report, a freshman in college who had traveled with the team told her remarkable story. She and another team member had entered a town with only a suitcase full of shoes. Though they thought they had brought enough for the people, especially the children, they were quickly overwhelmed with people lining up for whatever they had brought. Saying nothing to each other, they knew eventually the shoes would run out and people would have to be turned away. Not unlike my experience with the blind woman in Ukraine, the college student telling the story told us she breathed out less of a prayer than a question to God: "You see what's about to happen, right God?"

She and her partner started handing out shoes and kept handing out shoes and kept handing out shoes until finally there was no one left in line. It was only then that she inspected the suitcase. It was still full of shoes. Somehow the shoes had multiplied just like the loaves and fishes for the crowd in the gospels. When she finished telling her story, there was complete silence, then an eruption of applause for God. Had a miracle of multiplication really happened in our day? There wasn't an alternate explanation. I was aware of similar things happening in Mozambique at the hands of the missionary Heidi Baker. In one case, God had multiplied the meager amount of food she and her team had prepared, and it fed an entire village. It's remarkable and joyous to hear about such miracles, but most of us know in our minds we'll never see such a thing.

The year following the multiplication of the shoes, I led the next team to Nicaragua. We followed the same pattern as previous teams, collecting supplies and carrying them with us to Managua. Similar to previous years, before leaving, we prayed over the items that God would ensure there were sufficient numbers for those that needed them. Once in Nicaragua, we followed a routine each day of going to a district of Managua, conducting children's ministry during the day, and then holding a worship service in the evening. It was so joyous being able to dance and sing and celebrate with the children, watching their eyes as they encountered the Gospel, some for the first time.

A Love Letter to Twentysomethings Everywhere

On this day, we brought toys for the kids as a kind of reward for their participation. When the program ended, we had the kids queue up in two lines to receive the toys. I paired myself with a college student; I would do my best to sort the toys into things that would appeal either to a boy or a girl, then hand them to my partner to give to the children. Once I had my piles sorted, I understood that we had many fewer toys for girls than boys. I was kicking myself that we hadn't noticed this while we were still in the States. But as with the team the previous year, we decided we would just hand out what we had until we ran out, quietly whispering the same question, "You see what's about to happen, right God?" The toys were sitting on a washing machine, and I was standing next to the machine while my co-worker sat in a chair to be nearer the children's height when he handed them the toys. Because of this, I could see the top of the washer, but my partner couldn't.

As each child came to us, I would quickly turn to the washing machine, grab an appropriate toy, and give it to the college student to hand to the child. Child after child came through the line, and about half of the children were girls. Soon the toys for the girls would run out. Yet, each time I turned toward the washer, the pile of toys for girls wasn't changing. I didn't think too much about it, but after many girls had gone through, we still had toys left in the pile. I smiled, sensing that God was up to something, just like the year before. I also had to laugh to myself because my co-worker didn't know what was going on. No one did, except for God and me.

After the last child came through the line, I looked at the piles of toys, and there were still toys for girls, in fact, about the same number as we'd started with. How kind of God to do that for these kids. I didn't share this insight with my co-worker or anyone on the team, instead preferring to do as Mary the mother of Jesus had done, treasuring what had taken place in my heart. I didn't divulge my secret until we were standing as a team before our church, giving them a report on the trip. It was at that point that I said, "I want to share with you something God did for us in Nicaragua that even the team doesn't know about." Everyone was astonished,

Unexpected Miracles

including the team, and especially the guy who had worked with me distributing the toys.

From these unique experiences with miracles, I came to understand that God often does the most miraculous things right under our noses—miracles that appear so mundane that we could almost miss them. Did the disciples comprehend what was happening during the feeding of the 5,000? Probably not. They were just holding baskets, handing out pieces of bread and fish, hoping not to be trampled by an angry mob when the food ran out. But it didn't. In all the examples I've given of healing and of multiplication, there were no thunderbolts or flashes of lightning. Witnessing a miracle and growing in our faith are a lot like growing up physically. Unless we're growing by inches over a few months, we don't notice what's happening until someone measures us and remarks about how much we've grown. It was only in the aftermath of the miracles, having seen the result and then telling the tale, that crowds gasped and hands clapped and hallelujahs were shouted. But by then, I'd already grown up.

6

Growing Up Together

I've DISCOVERED OVER THE years that it's possible to become part of the construction and fulfillment of promises in others' lives, to witness the process up close. Whether it's in the revealing of a promise, or it's helping bring the promise to fruition, these are exciting moments that make a faith imprint on our lives. In the early 2000s, the pastor at our church resigned, and as I've already recounted, the leadership brought another pastor out of retirement to fill the pulpit for a year. He had a fire that we hadn't seen at the church for a long time, and he was eager to talk about the ministry of the Holy Spirit at every opportunity. He would hold trainings for us on Wednesday evenings on topics such as hearing God's voice and the ministry of the Spirit. Once he thought we were ready, we would then stand at the front of the church following Sunday morning service, and people were directed to us for prayer. Requests for prayer might be very specific or vaguely general. No matter, we took each one seriously.

One Sunday, I was standing at the front with a woman from my small group at church. We had typical requests: finances, healing, relatives, and so forth. We enjoyed the opportunity to pray with brothers and sisters because no matter whether the prayer was answered on the spot or days later, at that moment it was pure encouragement for the one receiving prayer. Toward the end of our time that morning, a woman came up to us and talked a bit about her situation. Though the request was a bit rambling, the bottom line was that she was looking for direction from God for her life. It's an easy prayer to pray. Jesus says in John 10:27, "My sheep listen to my voice; I know them, and they follow me." God wants to lead us, but he also wants to communicate with us. The pastor taught us that listening was as important as asking—that at some point, we had to allow God to speak his truth into the noisiness of our lives. So, the three of us prayed, but we also listened. These moments of listening can be awkward. In the silence, it's possible to convince ourselves that, even if God hears our prayers, he is choosing to remain silent. My take on this is that our lives are so noisy that it takes a certain amount of time even to discern the words of God. So we waited.

After a few minutes, my prayer partner said to the woman, "I want to share a picture I believe God is giving to me. I don't know what it means, but maybe you will." She then described being lifted off the earth by God until she was up in space looking down on the planet. She asked whether that meant anything to the woman we were praying for—it didn't. However, it meant something to me. It's not unlike working on a jigsaw puzzle, where you get to a certain point and you simply can't see how the pieces fit together. But then someone comes along, and instantly, they recognize how to complete the puzzle. I gave my interpretation to the woman. I didn't have to ask whether it was significant to her because she was in tears. "How could you know that?" she asked. I couldn't, I assured her, but God could. The Shepherd had spoken his promise to his sheep, and he had given my prayer partner and me the rare privilege of carrying that promise from the throne room and delivering it personally to her.

The next story I want to share may sound strange to you (as if the others haven't). My wife and I had the privilege of sitting under the teaching of our interim pastor for a full year, and during that time, he taught us about ministry of the Spirit using activation exercises, normally in small groups. He mostly intended the

A Love Letter to Twentysomethings Everywhere

exercises to get us to listen for the voice of God and then share with others as a way of encouraging them.

In one exercise we were in groups of three praying for each other, but we were asked only to pray out loud when we believed we'd heard from God. It might be a verse, a phrase, or even a mental picture. The pastor would group us with others that we did not know well, so we wouldn't be influenced by what we already knew about them.

The pastor directed us to focus on the John 10:27 passage where Jesus says, "My sheep listen to my voice." He asked, "Is Jesus your Shepherd? Are you his sheep?" Then we were told, "It is the will of God that you hear his voice, so that you can obey him. You just need to listen with your spirit, and trust that he will speak to you in a way that is unique to you. We are going to practice this right now. God has some things to say to some people in this next hour, and I trust you want to know what those things are. Do you want to know?" The answer seemed pretty obvious, and we were excited to be part of the process.

In each group, two people pray for one, for eight minutes, then shift to the next person and have the other two pray for that person, for eight minutes, and then repeat for the last person. We were simply to make ourselves available as God's vessel or instrument for that person's blessing. The results were remarkable, and the experience deeply affected my wife and me. We determined to carry the exercises with us to Ukraine and afford those we encountered in classes or individually with the same opportunity to hear God's voice.

I decided to take a chance and try out the listening prayer exercise on the first group I encountered during a teacher conference. Though skeptical, they were game to give it a try. There were many revelations that day, but none more impactful than one group of three that included one of our institute administrators. Whereas most of the teachers were from either a Pentecostal or Charismatic background, she was Baptist and had been all her life. For her, this exercise was like wading into the deep water, and she wasn't sure at all about the legitimacy of listening for God's voice, let alone sharing with others what she'd heard. Despite this, she joined two others from the conference, and when it was their turn, she and another woman prayed for the third person in their group.

In this exercise, there's a lot of silence, and we encourage this. We're so used to filling the space in prayer with our own voices. But in this case, we didn't want people to pray out of their heads; instead, we wanted the prayers to come from their spirits. The exercise went on for the requisite twenty-four minutes, and then, it was time for whomever wanted to share their reflections of what had happened. It astounded people that the prayers were so personal and specific, but even more surprising to some was experiencing hearing the voice of God for themselves, some for the first time. The sharing was joyful, and they gave God the glory over and over.

Then, shyly, the administrator put up her hand to speak. I was a little surprised at this, suspecting she might throw some shade on the proceedings, complaining about what a waste of time it had been. Nothing could have prepared me for what she said. She told us she and a woman had been praying, when suddenly the woman began to pray in tongues. Though the administrator had heard of this being done before, she had never witnessed it herself. Did she panic? A little, she said, just at first. Then a remarkable, even miraculous thing happened: In a moment of revelation she understood, with absolute certainty, that she had the interpretation.

As unusual as this is, it's definitely biblical. The Apostle Paul instructs the Corinthian believers, "I wish you could all speak in tongues, but even more I wish you could all prophesy. For prophecy is greater than speaking in tongues, unless someone interprets what you are saying so that the whole church will be strengthened" (1 Cor 14:5). So, this Baptist administrator took a deep breath and told the woman being prayed for, "I think I know the meaning of what she said." As was so often the case in these exercises, the word was particular for her circumstances (which were unknown to those praying) and encouraging for her spirit. The two praying individuals had been allowed to enter a promise, to carry a word of hope from God, wrapped in the very unusual package of tongues and interpretation. Even more, though, they had been allowed to

A Love Letter to Twentysomethings Everywhere

grow up spiritually, to understand that they were worthy of hearing the voice of God.

I'm sure we can agree that all of God's promises, however we receive them, are precious, and that the fulfillment of those promises is cause for celebration. But sometimes, God invites us to enter another person's private promise that has already been given to them and facilitate its fulfillment in their life. That happened with me while in Ukraine, and I consider it a high water mark of my life.

My then-assistant, Valya, was and is a remarkable woman. I'm convinced that, if not for her presence in the institute, the organization would have closed down years earlier. Her organizational and motivational skills are only surpassed by her spiritual gifting, in particular, her gift of discernment. God knew I needed her as my assistant because discernment is a gift I lack. I take everyone and everything at face value, and in Ukraine, that can be a risky way to live. Valya can sense whether a situation or person is safe or dangerous. In the movies this is called a sixth or Spidey sense, but I considered it to be directly from God.

Part of that gifting was the ability to know when to share information, when people were ready to hear it, or when to hold on to it for later. I learned from her that being led by the Spirit involves not only doing the right thing for the right reason, but also doing it at the right time. For Valya, timing was everything, because if God wasn't in it, she didn't want to have any part of it. Four years before I arrived in Ukraine, in 1998, a leadership conference was held in Poland. Among the downloads Valya received from God at the conference, the most surprising was a promise that she would write a book about her life. Now, understand that at that point Valya was only twenty years old and had just left home two years prior. She thought, as we all would, "What would I write about?" Still, she knew the promise was for her, and she held onto it, telling no one.

Fast forward to 2004, I'd become the director of the institute, and I'd worked with Valya for two years. Even if we know individuals well as colleagues, often we're more aware of their present than their past. Still, since her history was so closely tied to that of the institute, when she would talk about the first years of the organization, she would inevitably reveal some of her story as well. And, a lot had happened in the years since the 1998 conference in Poland, both miraculous and scandalous. The more I heard, the more amazed I was, and there was a growing sense in me that Valya should write a book about her experiences. It was apparent that she could write the book in Russian, her native language, but my concern was that it would have limited readership. Better, I thought, that she would write the book in English. However, this would be problematic because, though she could speak English well, Valya didn't write in English much at all.

As I processed these thoughts throughout the spring and summer of 2004, I realized I should offer to help her write her book in English, even though my experience with writing up to that point was solely academic. A day came when we were on an errand together in Kyiv, just walking and talking on a street near the office. I can see the scene now as if it just happened. It was cold enough to be wearing a coat; Valya's was long and black with a hood. The hood was up as we were walking along the street, so that when she looked over at me, the hood would partially obscure her face. We were just crossing at a street light when I dropped the bomb on her: "I think you should write a book about your life, and I think I should help you write it." She stopped in the middle of the crosswalk with a look on her face of utter shock. I had to take her arm to help her get to the other side. At first, she could hardly talk. But, finally, she shared with me the promise from God that she had kept locked away for six years. Then it was my turn to stare in disbelief.

We spent about three months writing, grabbing an hour here and there at the end of the workday. At that very moment, the country of Ukraine was in upheaval. It was discovered the presidential election and subsequent runoff were rigged, resulting in hundreds of thousands of Ukrainians from all over the country descending on Kyiv to protest the outcome. It came to be known as the Orange Revolution, the color of the opposition party. Offices across the city set up rotations of their workers, so that some would be manning the office, some would be in the city square, and some would be on their way to the square or returning from it. My institute office was no different; it was absolutely electric. Some days a few from the office would go to the square—other days we just closed up shop so that everyone could go. Because the office environment was more fluid than normal, there was time to work on the book.

I'd sit in front of the office computer transcribing what Valya told me, asking for clarification or additional information so that her verbal retelling could be read on a page. Although we were writing her autobiography, and despite her willingness to tell the whole unvarnished truth, there were stories she would tell me, but then say, she didn't want to include them in the book. I'd plead with her, but she was resolute.

One story she did include was about her father's death and funeral, which took place when she was only a teenager. She described in painstaking detail having the body lying in state in the living room of her house (a Ukrainian tradition) and fearing to walk around the body to go through the front door. The details of her recollection, down to the smells, were so vivid it was like I was there with her. I had also lost my father about ten years earlier, and her description of standing next to the coffin, of coming to terms with such a devastating loss, hit close to home. Her last words to her father were, "I know it won't help to kiss you because you can't feel my love."[1]

After I typed those words, we both sat in silence, each remembering the passing of our fathers, each amazed at what had transpired since then to allow a twentysomething Ukrainian to dictate a book about her life to an American. It was one of the most holy moments I'd experienced, when the presence of God was tangible all around us. I sensed his pleasure with the book, and we both grew up that day, albeit in different ways. We were witnessing the fulfillment of a promise that had seemed impossible to Valya only six years earlier, and that I'd judged myself unqualified to facilitate only a few months before. Those are the days when growing up can be pure joy.

1. Grenchuk & Shotsberger, *My Father Loves Me*, 53

January 2005 was the culmination not only of the dictation for the book but also the Orange Revolution, as the opposition candidate was sworn in as the new president of Ukraine. Those were heady days. Because the institute printed its own books for use in Bible schools, there was already a mechanism in place for getting Valya's book published. We coordinated with a printing house in western Ukraine that we used regularly, and in short order, we had 1,000 copies printed and ready for distribution.

God knew how timely the publication of the book would be. In the next few years, Valya would have many opportunities to travel to other countries, including the United States, and the book became the centerpiece of her presentations to churches. I have a sweet picture of Valya, following a talk in Texas, sitting on the steps of the stage with an older gentleman man autographing a copy of her book for him. The book was an introduction not only to Valya's life and times, but also to Ukrainian culture and tradition. It made life in Ukraine more relatable to people from other countries, resulting in increased support for the work of the institute.

By 2009, my wife and I were ready to return to the United States permanently, and there was only one candidate to replace me as director: Valya. Never one to shy away from a challenge, she embraced the work, and the institute became even stronger with her at the helm. This is the verse she has chosen to live by, which she insisted be put on the back cover of her book:

> Don't be afraid, for I am with you.
> Don't be discouraged, for I am your God.
> I will strengthen you and help you.
> I will hold you up with my victorious right hand. (Isa 41:10)

Valya now lives in the United States and is the operations director for my former missions agency, overseeing the work of many ministries and educational organizations around the world. Similar to my own life, God has been faithful to keep his promises to Valya, allowing her to mature into the leader he needs for his Kingdom work.

7

Protection and Provision

I'VE DEPENDED ON GOD'S grace my entire life. I'm not one to assume too much about my own abilities and so get caught up in a cycle of self-sufficiency. But, I'm also not the most careful person, and so I've found myself in situations where I'm trapped and in need of God's protection and provision. These can be terrifying times, but also the kinds that lend themselves to growing up.

I had the sense even as a child that God's safeguarding hand was on me, a kind of lifelong promissory note giving me deep assurance amid questionable and even dangerous circumstances. I've already recounted my years-long struggle with bullies growing up. Though we can minimize those times from the perspective of an adult, as a child our tormentors are terrorists and we see ourselves in great danger. Yet, there have been circumstances in my life that anyone at any age would agree were perilous or threatening, some of my own making but many through no fault of my own. Each time, God kept his promise of protection.

For some of my time growing up, I lived in the hills of northern New Jersey. These were the last exhilarating days of high school, driving my friends around in my family's Audi 100, a sweet little sporty sedan. One night, a friend and I had just eaten dinner at a wonderful restaurant called O'Connor's, a favorite among my friends, and we were driving back home in the rain.

Protection and Provision

The Watchung Mountains have lots of twisting and turning roads, and with my new license and my still-forming prefrontal cortex, I was driving way too fast for the conditions. We came around a sharp turn high in the hills, overlooking a ravine, and I was suddenly aware of the momentum we were carrying. To compensate, I turned the wheel harder, desperately trying to meet the turn. Then it happened. For just a split second, one side of the car seemed to lift up from the road. In that moment, as time slowed down, I turned to look at my friend, and it was obvious from his eyes that we were thinking the same thing: we won't make this turn.

I've often looked back on that moment as a metaphor for all the times that I've been backed into a corner with no way out and yet have sensed God's presence with me. It's almost as if he's saying, "I've still got more for you." When I was little, I had a strong sense of being unusual. I was sure that everyone but me was a robot, as if I was living in some science fiction world. Yet, there was hope for the robots. As I came to know them, even simply greeting them or our eyes meeting on the street, they'd magically turn into flesh and blood humans. That, in a nutshell, was how special I considered myself. God saw me as different, someone requiring exceptional treatment. I was his agent in the world, giving those poor robots a chance at life. If today you are a flesh-and-blood human being and not a robot, you're welcome. Though I was nothing special to look at and could easily get lost in a crowd, God thought of me as someone worth protecting. He thinks of you in exactly the same way.

Since I'm writing these words to you many years after the two-wheel incident in high school, we obviously made it around the turn. Despite our special status in God's eyes, one important aspect of becoming an adult is the need to dispense with a sense of invulnerability. Besides developing a fully formed prefrontal cortex that warns us away from danger, the other part of growing up is deeply psychological and even spiritual: coming to grips with our own mortality and realizing where our hope for this life lies. It's then that the words of Psalm 91:14–16 come alive:

A Love Letter to Twentysomethings Everywhere

> The Lord says, "I will rescue those who love me.
> I will protect those who trust in my name.
> When they call on me, I will answer;
> I will be with them in trouble.
> I will rescue and honor them.
> I will reward them with a long life
> and give them my salvation."

The sensation of helplessness coupled with reassurance has never left me. I had that same feeling a few years after my near-accident, at the age of twenty-four, sitting at anchor aboard my Navy ship in Beirut harbor. Because of the training I had received in helicopter flight operations, I was one of only two primary flight officers aboard. This meant that I'd sit for hours on end in a little metal and Plexiglas shack, known as primary flight control or pri-fly, and direct the helicopters bringing needed supplies and reinforcements to the Marines ashore.

I gained great satisfaction from this job, especially enjoying the easy banter with the pilots over the radio. Much as with writing a letter to someone you'd never met, we would begin formally: "Bravo-two-Lima, this is Sierra-one-Victor, over." But after a few exchanges it became more informal, "Roger, Two-Lima," and then finally, just two squeezes of the push-to-talk button in my hand: *bump-bump*. My hope of being a pilot in the Navy never materialized,[1] but at least in this world I was the pilot's equal. There was nowhere I'd rather be aboard ship, even when watches in pri-fly stretched on for two, three, or four hours at a time. It helped that I was never alone in the shack; I had a small cadre of enlisted men who manned the sound-powered telephones to various parts of the ship: the bridge, the flight deck, and below decks.

On one particularly busy day, we were in our cramped quarters, engulfed in a din of talk and activity. You've probably had the experience of hearing an unusual noise in an otherwise familiar setting—it can be unsettling. Amid the usual noises of pri-fly, we heard a *whoosh* pass over the little building. We were up high on the ship, overlooking the flight deck, so it was difficult to process

---

1. Shotsberger, *Moments that Matter*, 11–14.

where the sound had come from. I asked a sailor on duty with me to go outside and find out what had happened. He returned a minute later looking pale.

"What was it?" I asked.

"A missile," he told me.

Apparently, a Lebanese helicopter hovering near us had accidentally released a missile, and it had passed just feet above our heads. Those of us in the shack looked at each other with much the same expression as my friend and I had that night in the Watchung Mountains: no smiles, no laughter, almost in disbelief over our near-miss. Promise fulfilled, again.

That same promise has also manifested itself as provision for myself and my family, many times over. Our first year as missionaries in Ukraine, we rented an apartment that was suitable for our needs, but didn't feel like home. Half way through that year, we decided to stay in Ukraine long term and so sold our dream house in the United States. Suddenly, my wife and I were debt free for the first time in our marriage, and it was a glorious feeling. But a reality of being an adult is taxes, and we came to understand that unless we reinvested our gains, we'd get socked with an enormous tax bill. So we weighed a major decision for missionaries: the possibility of home ownership in a foreign country, with its Communist-era laws and restrictions.

There were houses we could purchase outside of Kyiv, but we wanted to stay in the city where we could have easier access to my office and our son's school. We asked my assistant in the office, Valya, to look around for apartments for purchase. It wasn't too long before she found the perfect place, on the ninth floor of an apartment building intended exclusively to house families of KGB workers during the days of the Soviet Union. Though the restriction on occupancy had loosened somewhat, there were still government employees living in the building. (I sometimes rode the elevator in the morning with an affable and inquisitive man who showed a keen interest in why an American would be living in his building.) The government connection meant that the building was clean and kept up, and come winter the snow would be cleared from the sidewalks and parking lot. There was easy access to the supermarket, metro, and bus for our son's school. The apartment also had a beautiful view of the Dnipro River to the east.

We bought the apartment in 2003 for $60,000. We were told by other Americans we were crazy, that the price was much too high, and that we'd never get our money back. Most missionaries were renting—they saw it as a way to stay lithe and unencumbered in their ministry. But a foreigner buying property meant something special to Ukrainians. We were invested and there for the long term. The apartment had two bedrooms, and though it was only 720 square feet, it was spacious by Ukrainian standards. It was perfect for our small family of three, warm and inviting for Ukrainians and Americans alike. (The Ukrainians fancied it a palace; the Americans felt sorry for us.) We celebrated holidays there, including the first Thanksgiving dinner my Ukrainian staff had ever experienced. We had our son's friends and American visitors stay with us regularly. My wife also had a group of teenage girls come over weekly to do decorative stamping with her, partly as a ministry and partly as a business. Many of those who visited our apartment considered it their second home.

In 2009 we returned to the United States, but we didn't sell the apartment right away, partly because the Great Recession had just begun the year before. Instead, we rented it for a year to a young couple teaching at our son's former school where he had graduated in 2007. In 2010, after the economy had recovered somewhat, we were ready to sell, but we weren't at all sure what the apartment was worth at that point. Valya searched diligently until she found a buyer, a man who wanted a place for his parents. She was also looking for an apartment the institute could purchase to use as a newer, larger office space. We worked out a scheme wherein we would use some proceeds of the sale of our apartment, as both gift and loan, to purchase the office. But, of course, that purchase was contingent on our apartment selling.

We planned to come to Kyiv for a week to close the deal in person. We knew we had to have the original proof of purchase for the apartment with us, which we had translated and notarized.

Protection and Provision

Just days before we left the States for Ukraine, Valya surprised us by saying we also needed an apostille, which is a certification of a notary signature from the state of residence. We were to leave for Ukraine on Friday and only received word of the apostille on Wednesday. There was no time to secure the document.

When we showed up at the lawyer's office in Kyiv the following Monday with only the notarized proof of purchase, we were told flatly there was no way to close the deal without the apostille. Ukrainians suspect each other's motives, due primarily to seventy years under Communist rule. So, in typical Ukrainian fashion, they also accused us of trying to drive up the price of the sale by delaying the transaction. After a lot of back and forth, the lawyer suggested we could go to the US embassy in Kyiv and get a statement of authenticity from them. This, of course, required an appointment that we couldn't get until Wednesday, and our departure back to the USA was scheduled for Friday. But even then, what could the embassy do for us? They had no power to issue an apostille, and it seemed little else mattered to the lawyer.

The morning of the appointment, I sat alone in the kitchen of our apartment. The couple who had rented from us had already moved out, and the previous year we'd taken most of our belongings to the United States, so there was little left. On a small shelf sat our CD player, but of course, the CDs had all been moved out. Or, so I thought. It surprised me to find a CD in the player that everyone except God had forgotten about. It was the Delirious? album *World Service*. I was without hope at that point. I imagined the embassy telling us there was nothing they could do, the lawyer would therefore say, "too bad, so sad," the institute would be without a larger office space, and we'd fly home the proud owners of an empty apartment in Kyiv. The one thing I had left was worship. As with David in the Psalms, if I had nothing else and if everything looked hopeless, I could still worship. And so I did, as song after song played on the CD. Finally came the last song, "Everything Little Thing," with its repeated chorus, "Every little thing's gonna be alright." I'd always thought the chorus insipid, a hackneyed sentiment that bore no relation to reality. Yet, in that sacred moment in the kitchen of

55

A Love Letter to Twentysomethings Everywhere

the apartment I so desperately needed to sell, God was speaking a promise directly to my heart. I had a supernatural peace come over me, and for the first time that week, I experienced hope.

We went to the embassy, and the representative told us exactly what we expected: They couldn't authenticate a signed document, and they couldn't help us with our problem. My wife and I sat there absorbing the news. But then God nudged the man, and he suggested a crazy idea. What the embassy could do was make a copy of what we already had and stamp it as a certified authentic copy. This, to me, sounded like a joke, because the lawyer was demanding the certification of the original, not a copy. Yet, the representative was Ukrainian, and to him, it made sense. And of course, it's all we had.

We took the certified copy and rushed to the lawyer's office, expecting to be laughed out onto the street. Impossibly, the lawyer accepted the document just as if it had been an apostille. He quickly called a meeting of all the parties for Thursday afternoon at the buyer's bank, less than twenty-four hours before our scheduled departure for the USA. We settled on a final selling price that was three times what we'd paid for the apartment originally. So much for the naysayers. Though I believed with all my heart that God could accomplish the impossible task of a successful exchange, I was still holding my breath, waiting for the deal to fall through on a technicality (such faith, right?). But, it didn't.

Like so much that happens in Ukraine, the sale was a cash transaction. Susan, Valya, and I had the surreal experience of opening banded packets of brand new hundred-dollar bills, and counting out the purchase amount to ensure it was all there. We then handed the lawyer his commission plus the taxes and fees he would pay on our behalf and signed the remaining papers. At that point, I exhaled for the first time that whole week.

But we weren't quite finished because we also had to go across town to deposit most of the money in another bank for the purchase of the institute's new office space. We would take the balance with us to the United States. In Kyiv, at least in those days, you didn't simply call a taxi service. You stopped a car on the street and

Protection and Provision

asked if they would take you where you needed to go, negotiating a fare for the trip. So, that's what we did. There I was, riding across town in a stranger's car with over $100,000 in cash in my shoulder bag, hoping we didn't get stopped by the police, all the while grinning a grin that wouldn't go away. God had kept his promise that "Every little thing's gonna be alright."

Before I end this chapter, allow me a moment to talk about the timing of God. In my book *Choices*, I make this statement: "We are led by the Spirit when we do the right thing for the right reason at the right time. It is not simply a matter of doing the right thing, or even doing the right thing for the right reason."[2] We had purchased the apartment at the beginning of our second year in Ukraine, a decision that was validated many times over in the years we lived there. We were convinced we'd done the right thing for the right reason. And we had promises from God, first for coming to Ukraine, and then for departing and, ultimately, for selling the apartment. So, we believed we were in God's timing then as well, not only for us but also for the institute that needed finances for a permanent office space. In every way, we could say with confidence we were being led by the Spirit.

Yet, the timing we imagined for the sale was still not quite God's timing. Here is a revelation that I have slowly come to grips with over my lifetime: the promises of God aren't actually for us, but for God, for his purposes, and for his glory. I'll go a step further and say that our God not only wants glory, he wants *maximum* glory. He wants the glory that results from a promise kept in the fullness of time, which sometimes means in extremis.

If we'd received the notice in plenty of time to get the apostille and had waltzed into the lawyer's office and made his day by handing him everything we needed the very first time, there would have been glory for God, but nothing like the glory given by us when we witnessed the impossible. This is something God seeks from us and even occasionally manufactures from our circumstances. It's not what we would choose—it's not convenient or comfortable, but it's always memorable. Like an Ebenezer, a stone of remembrance,

2. Shotsberger, *Choices*, 7.

A Love Letter to Twentysomethings Everywhere

we can return to it over and over to remind us we serve a faithful God. That bit of discomfort we experience pales against the exuberant triumph of a promise fulfilled. And we worship, over and over, every time we think about that incident. It's a glorious thing to behold, again and again.

But what of growing up? I received a master's degree in how the world works from my experience in selling the apartment, but that doesn't mean I grew up. There are many worldly-wise people who understand the system and can make it work for them, but they're spiritually underdeveloped despite, and sometimes because of, their experience. The more we learn, the more self-reliant we can become, stunting our own spiritual growth. The trick is to go through the experience, learning our lessons, while also staying humble and dependent on God's will and timing.

Once we dig in our heels and demand to do things our way, we've lost whatever opportunity existed to grow up; we've co-opted God's promise and made ourselves into the only one who can fulfill it. This is a dangerous place to be because we're essentially placing ourselves above our Maker, and we know from the first commandment that this is something abhorrent to God (Ex 20:3). So, did I grow up the day we sold the apartment? Yes, but also the previous day at the embassy, and that morning in the kitchen, and the first disappointing day in the lawyer's office, and the day we found out we needed an apostille but couldn't get one. Every time I faced discouraging (and worse) circumstances and still looked to God for answers, I grew up. It's that simple and that complicated; it's that easy and that hard; it's that desperate and that glorious. And it's so worth it.

8

You're Never Too Young or Too Old

WE'RE MISTAKEN WHEN WE think we're too young or too old to grow up. When we're younger, we think everyone is more mature and put together than we are. What business do we have trying to act like an adult? As we age, though, the challenge becomes change. It's difficult to describe the threat that change becomes—we come to value predictability and comfort. At that point, growing up looks like pure sacrifice, and we resent it. This chapter is about both of those times.

As an illustration of a twentysomething who seized the opportunity to grow up, I'd like to introduce you to a former student of mine. Her name is Sarah, and she was only twenty-one when she died in a violent car crash. In almost forty years of teaching, I have rarely been so impacted by a student. When she arrived the first day of my ethics course, she immediately headed for a seat in the back row of the classroom. We all make judgments about others based on precious little information. My snap judgment that day was that this was someone who would prefer to be left alone, but I couldn't have been more wrong. Sarah was always prepared for class, but more than simply doing the required reading, she actually had thought deeply about the implications of what she'd read. Every class, her eyes were locked on me as I lectured. Her hand was raised with questions she had, and when asked her

A Love Letter to Twentysomethings Everywhere

opinion, she offered her observations easily, in an informed way that seemed to come from someone much older.

Most students who take my ethics course are undergraduate education majors, meaning that they're on their way to a teaching career of some description, and Sarah was an early childhood major. I ask students in the course to personalize what they're learning, deciding on an ethic for themselves that they can apply and defend in their own teaching. The capstone project of the course is a personal ethics paper asking students to choose ethical theories from their reading and justify the choice as the basis of their own morality. Sarah had been a delight throughout the semester, yet despite the depth of consideration I'd witnessed, I was caught off guard by her final paper. Her honesty, reasoning, and commitment to teaching were refreshing and energizing for this old professor. I want to share just a bit of what she wrote, as a way of honoring her memory while also allowing her life to inspire others, the way she hoped to inspire her future students. I also want to share my experience of attending her memorial service as a way of talking about the profound changes we can make when we're in our twenties.

Sarah began the paper by sharing about her first day at my university. She had transferred from a technical college, and this would be her first time attending a Christian school of any kind. So, she didn't know what to expect, but she was excited about the possibilities. Sarah was driving to campus when she received a call from her cousin. They talked often, and she assumed this was just a check-in as she headed into classes. Instead, she heard the unimaginable news that their mutual friend had passed away from a heart attack the night before. He was only twenty years old when he died, and she was writing her paper about eight months after his death. She described the overwhelming grief weighing on her as she walked into her first class, and the care she experienced from her professor as he prayed for the class that morning. Personal ethics papers are long, filled with ethical theory and application, as well as personal reflection. It's difficult to capture such a paper in a few sentences, but I have tried. I'll step aside now and let Sarah speak for herself:

You're Never Too Young or Too Old

I am in no way saying that [the friend's] death happened for the sole purpose of me understanding my want to become a great teacher; I am also still not entirely sure what the reason behind such an incredible person leaving this Earth so young even is. I do know . . . I was meant to be at that low point in order to see what God wanted from me. He knew what He was doing that morning even if I was completely blindsided by it . . . I want to be able to guide my students in any situation the way I would try and handle it. I think this is an exciting and very important aspect of being a great teacher, to be able to show your students the respect you give to yourself . . . Showing respect for your students will allow them to express themselves and even allow them to deal with problems by talking it out and knowing you are there to listen not judge . . . I have learned this semester that it is very important for a teacher to develop their own thoughts and feelings on the different ethical theories in order for them to have the motivation and want to help their students and community around them. Without a reason or a passion behind what you do you will never truly give it your all . . . I am incredibly thankful for my time at [the university] and the way God is working in my life. Even [in] small things I can still see Him moving in my life, pushing me to do my best, and even when I feel so alone that there is someone there for me all the time.

Sarah died almost exactly one year after she completed my course. When I read the news, I sat at my computer and wept. I revisited her personal ethics paper and was struck with the irony of reading about the loss of her friend even as I was mourning her death. My reaction was the same as hers when she was told about the death of her friend: The tragedy was inexplicable. Such a promising life—what a wonderful teacher she would have been. I wanted to honor her and represent my university at her memorial service, but I was unprepared for what I encountered.

A large picture of a young Sarah with brown hair stood on an easel in the church's foyer; my student had been blond. Those who spoke about her, including her father, talked as if she was

A Love Letter to Twentysomethings Everywhere

still a child and somewhat flighty; the person I had known was analytical, serious, and a passionate professional-in-the-making. The memorial was filled with testimonies about a person that bore no relation to the student I'd taught. Then it struck me: at the age of twenty or so, she had decided to become an adult. This was in part because of the tragedy of losing her friend, in part because of the care shown to her by God and her professors, and in part because of a conscious decision to be the best educator she could be. These characteristics were alien to those who had known her only as the daughter or the girl next door. I'll always be grateful for having known Sarah when I did, the twentysomething young woman comfortable in her skin, already an adult.

So, we're never too young to grow up, but we're also never too old. And that brings me to a recent opportunity God granted me to do just that, even as I was teetering on the edge of sixty. After spending seven years in Ukraine, I had taken an education professor position at Southern Wesleyan University in South Carolina. Though my primary duties were as dean of the school of education, because of my background I was also helping to coordinate the math education program. Part and parcel of this was teaching math courses. By 2017, I'd been teaching math in some capacity for thirty-five years, everything from pre-algebra to A.P. Calculus in high school, and from Calculus I and geometry to a math history course in college. Math was my jam.

For the uninitiated, or those who in fact hate math, it's difficult to describe how it gets into your system. Once, at my former university, offices in the math department where I worked were being painted, so whiteboards were taken off the walls and put in the hallway. I was walking down the hall one day and glanced at one board full of mathematics. I smiled and said to no one in particular, "How cool is that?" Math was to be regarded and never taken for granted, because just at the moment you thought you understood, you came across a question that made you have to dive back into the theorems and corollaries all over again, searching for an answer. It was a never-ending journey, and I loved it.

You're Never Too Young or Too Old

I loved the beauty and complexity of it, yet I was confident that anyone could engage with it given sufficient curiosity and support. Along the way, I had the privilege of teaching students who were brighter than me, who inspired me to dig deeper into familiar terrain to find the gold that lay buried beneath. I did not view most of what I taught in the education field the same way—for me, it was the difference between adventure and apprenticeship. With sufficient experience, it's nearly a sure bet the apprentice will become a master, though probably not in the first few years. I'd prepare the education candidates the best I could, assess their tentative attempts as novice teachers, and hope for the best as they crossed the stage to receive their diplomas and go on to teaching careers.

But with math, it wasn't so much about the future as it was about the present. In the present, there was wonder and deep accomplishment. Students were less apprentices and more adventurers, fully capable of uncovering the most remarkable results. Yes, it's true that most of what they unearthed had been discovered hundreds and even thousands of years prior, but that hardly mattered. In that moment they were mathematicians, a deeply satisfying place to be. But after many years of being part of thriving math and math education programs at two different universities, by the mid-2010s the spigot it seemed was being shut off by an unseen hand. Fewer students were choosing to follow the arduous path of secondary education in order to be certified, opting instead for alternative certification. By 2017, we had to make the tough decision to end all secondary education programs at my university. These were the very programs that allowed the liberal art of math to thrive, and so demand for those courses dropped precipitously.

At the same time, my school of education was making plans for a doctorate related to my specialization of Curriculum and Instruction. I was being asked to transition from math education to coordinating the doctoral program, which was still in utero. Although the handwriting was on the wall for math and math education, teaching those courses had been part of my life for my entire career as a professor. Though I can look back now and see God's guiding hand in the transition, this opportunity to grow up

A Love Letter to Twentysomethings Everywhere

seemed like being robbed of something precious, an uneven trade that would require me to administer and teach courses that lacked adventure and discovery.

Sometimes, no, most times, growing up is like that. We all imagine when we're young that being an adult means freedom and independence, but we fail to factor in the responsibilities required of us. This is where the whole "We Can't Adult" thing comes from. As Fredrick Backman says in his excellent novel *Anxious People*, "When you're a child you long to be an adult and decide everything for yourself, but when you're an adult you realize that's the worst part of it."[1]

The dean who was requiring me to make the transition had been my associate dean during the four years I headed the school of education. We had worked well together, and when I stopped being a dean, she was the only choice for the job. The most remarkable thing about her is her uncanny ability to look into the future, figure out what will be needed of education five or ten years into the future, and then go about creating programs or courses to meet that need. When she came up with the idea for the doctorate, no one could have expected the COVID-19 pandemic and the detrimental impact it would have on education, and specifically, higher education.

Similar to most other universities, our enrollments fell off a cliff, and it seemed few programs or personnel were spared a drastic winnowing. One of the few exceptions was the doctorate. It seemed no matter how challenging the times were, especially for K-12 teachers and administrators, there was still keen interest in the program. The dean had also foreseen the need to compensate faculty for their service on dissertation committees. Thus, once the pay cuts and mandatory furloughs started at my university to shore up a sagging budget, I was insulated more than most of my colleagues.

I could have hung on to my precious math and math education courses and/or fought moving to the doctoral program, but I would have been working against God's plan for me. We do this,

---

1. Backman, *Anxious People*, 184.

don't we? We imagine we know better than God, and that whatever we have accomplished for ourselves is better than the fulfillment of God's promise of care and guidance in our lives. David declared in Psalm 23 that the Lord was his Shepherd, and to drive home the fact that this wasn't just a title, he delineated what that meant for his life: rest, restoration, assurance, companionship, comfort, abundance, protection, and eternal security. Jesus proclaims in the gospels that he is the Good Shepherd, and that beyond providing for us as he did for David, he was willing to die for us. The frosting on the cake is that God has a plan and a future for us.

Why do we think that this future God has for us is less than the one we can provide for ourselves? Yet, this was the original sin, wasn't it? God had provided everything Adam and Eve needed for a perfect life, but they reached out for the one thing God told them would kill them. Every time we take matters into our own hands and live our lives as though the fulfillment of God's promises is up to us, we set ourselves up for failure. The price of that failure may be judgment, but it may simply mean that we're stuck where we are, unable to grow up, repeating the same mistakes over and over. Do you know an adult who acts like a toddler, throwing tantrums and demanding their own way? Psychologically, these people are acting out of their emotional age. Some people are stunted in their emotional age because of trauma, but some, I'm convinced, have settled on an age when they believed they still had control of their lives, and they've chosen to live their remaining days at that emotional age.

The multi-billion-dollar industry called College Football targets those who have decided that college was the best time of their lives and who seek to relive those halcyon days before, during, and after every game their university's team plays. So, people spend way too much on tailgating, including catering and satellite television, they drink far too much, and they act as if they're still underage (I know that's a gross generalization and there are many exceptions, but there are many more who fit the definition). This aberrant behavior is considered by them to be the epitome of freedom. My insight from observing this behavior for many years is

A Love Letter to Twentysomethings Everywhere

that these are the same people who say they "can't adult," and this is how they cope. It's the Peter Pan Syndrome, the refusal to grow up.

A biblical example of this unwillingness or inability to grow into responsible adulthood is King Saul, the hapless first king of Israel. From a worldly standpoint, what was it that qualified Saul for the throne? Basically, he was tall, dark, and handsome, but we see from the outset the emotional age he acted out of, as first evidenced when he was to be introduced to the nation. God had identified him as his choice for king, and Samuel had already anointed him. So, where was he on his big day? Hiding among the Israelite baggage (which was foolish, since he was a head taller than everyone else). Can we pin down Saul's emotional age? Given his response to being announced as king, I'd say, in his mind, he was about seven or eight years old. His subsequent actions as king, which included lying, making excuses, emotional outbursts, and disregard for and disobedience of God's commands, confirm this.

Toward the beginning of his reign, God had commanded Saul to take a city and told him in no uncertain terms that he should leave nothing alive. However, Saul held out some animals for himself, as well as spared the king. In fact, we're told, ". . . They destroyed only what was worthless or of poor quality" (1 Sam 15:9). Oops. When confronted by Samuel, who plays the part of the exasperated parent, first Saul lies, and then when presented with evidence of his disobedience he makes excuses:

> When Samuel finally found him, Saul greeted him cheerfully. "May the Lord bless you," he said. "I have carried out the Lord's command!" "Then what is all the bleating of sheep and goats and the lowing of cattle I hear?" Samuel demanded. "It's true that the army spared the best of the sheep, goats, and cattle," Saul admitted. "But they are going to sacrifice them to the Lord your God. We have destroyed everything else." (1 Sam 15:13–15)

Just like a little kid. Parents endure many fanciful tales spun by a child caught red-handed, desperately wanting to avoid punishment. And this behavior grieves us. Why didn't they just do what were told to do? Why did the child have to lie to cover up their disobedience? So it was with Samuel, the erstwhile parent in the story. We hear the anguish of his heart in his words to Saul:

> And Samuel told him, "Although you may think little of yourself, are you not the leader of the tribes of Israel? The Lord has anointed you king of Israel. And the Lord sent you on a mission and told you, 'Go and completely destroy the sinners, the Amalekites, until they are all dead.' Why haven't you obeyed the Lord? Why did you rush for the plunder and do what was evil in the Lord's sight?" (1 Sam 15:17–19)

In other words, "Saul, you had the promises of God in your hand and you threw them away." Why? Because he wanted his own way. And why was that? Because he refused to mature into the anointing, the promise given to him. He couldn't, or wouldn't, "adult." The people expected much of him, but he just wasn't up to the task. The result was that God took the kingdom away from Saul and gave it to David. As noted previously, there's a popular saying that, "If God calls, he also equips." True enough, but we also have a part to play in that calling. That part includes, in large measure, growing up, not only emotionally but also spiritually. And that growing up can happen in our twenties or in our sixties.

There are many successful people, including many Christians, who can, in fact, "adult" just fine, but they have no interest in growing up spiritually. Of course, that reluctance makes perfect sense. Spiritual growth is predicated on surrender and humility, and for many that level of vulnerability is beyond the pale. Why put away the privileges of childhood in order to become a professional, as my student Sarah did? Why give up a passionate pursuit of math to become just some program coordinator, as I was required to do? I'll tell you why: Because people fail, and we fail ourselves, but God never fails. If everyone deserts us, if we stop believing in ourselves, Jesus is still our Good Shepherd. The psalmist put it succinctly:

> For that is what God is like.
> He is our God forever and ever,
> and he will guide us until we die. (Ps 48:14)

A Love Letter to Twentysomethings Everywhere

The hard truth about growing up is that, though it's obvious God does not desire and will not tolerate anything in our lives that displeases him, he also requires us to sacrifice to him the very giftings with which he has graced us. Much is said in Christian circles about avoiding birthing an Ishmael, the workaround born out of the schemes of humans rather than the promises of God. Much less is said about God's command to Abraham to sacrifice Isaac, the gift granted to Abraham in his old age.

God has to know that we've committed everything to him. We can't just confess our sins and grow up into the likeness of Christ; we have to do as Christ did and lay down our lives, including the beauty that God has baked into our souls. Perhaps God calls us to overseas missions, but it just so happens that we're tired of our humdrum lives. That's convenient, isn't it? All we have to do is give up the thing that we really wanted to jettison anyway. Are we ready to serve as a missionary now? Hardly.

Yet, if we will give our best to the Redeemer, he will always make something better from it. Childhood can be exchanged for a mature and inspiring life; personal passion can be transformed into something deeply meaningful and impactful. Sarah's parents and friends kept her young in their minds, ignoring the woman she was becoming. But, Sarah had other plans. She was becoming a new creation, taking on the mantle of teacher, exercising the developing judgment God had given her in order to think and act differently. The doctoral students didn't need my heart for math. They needed the thing I valued most from my own time as a doctoral candidate, the understanding and practice of research. And they needed an emerging interest I'd been developing in ethics. One was a spark that was unexpectedly but joyously rekindled; the other was a deep well of ideas that I'd only recently realized had the potential of affecting individuals in unexpected and profound ways. Research and ethics proved me wrong about education courses not allowing for discovery and adventure; I just had to sacrifice one love to find another.

Now, suppose I'd known the end-game for these sacrifices before making them. Would they have still been sacrifices? Yes, but the act of giving them up would have required no faith. Second only to worship, our God values our faith-filled obedience, the offer of the bird in our hand before knowing anything about the two in the bush. Sometimes the promises of God to us are explicit, such as the specific word given to me about the woman I would marry. But most times, the promises of God are open-ended, and yet, we need to obey anyway. Speaking about the law given to Moses, a testament that contains many promises, Peter Enns notes, "There's a lot at stake here, but rather than clarity we get ambiguity. The law as written leaves its readers to ponder what it means and how to obey it here and now—in other words, to practice wisdom."[2]

In the presence of ambiguity, what is the source of wisdom and the faith to grow up? It comes from what we know of our God, of the faithfulness he has shown in the past (both in Scripture and in our lives), and the rock solid promise Jesus gave to never leave us or forsake us. Recall the words of Jesus I quoted earlier: "No, I will not abandon you as orphans—I will come to you" (John 14:18). Perhaps I'm just simpleminded, but that's enough for me to strike out on the adventure God has for me, to follow his promises on the path to maturity, even if I think I'm too old—or you think you're too young. Is it enough for you?

---

2. Enns, *How The Bible Actually Works*, 56.

9

Responding to God's Voice

BEFORE CONCLUDING THIS BOOK, I want to talk about how we respond to God's voice, something I'm still learning. I taught a course in Ukraine called "Knowing God's Voice and Will." The textbook was *Knowing God's Voice* from the Harvestime International Network (harvestime.org); the book is freely available through the publisher, and I highly recommend it. The last chapter is called Six Stages of Revelation, and I want to present an adapted version of it here because the steps are helpful when we come face to face with God's promises. The chapter is based on Mary's encounter with the angel Gabriel in Luke 1 and breaks down nicely into steps or stages:

1. God gets our attention (vss. 28–29): "Gabriel appeared to her and said, 'Greetings, favored woman! The Lord is with you!' Confused and disturbed, Mary tried to think what the angel could mean." Events are taking place which are unfamiliar and troubling to us. Something is happening, but we don't understand it.

2. God gives us a revelation (or for this book, a promise) (vss. 30–31): "'Don't be afraid, Mary,' the angel told her, 'for you have found favor with God! You will conceive and give birth to a son, and you will name him Jesus.'" Once God has our

Responding to God's Voice

attention (often through circumstances), he reveals the "new thing" he is doing in our lives.

3. We respond with hesitation (vs. 34): "Mary asked the angel, 'But how can this happen? I am a virgin.'" At first, the revelation sounds like too much for us, primarily, because we're thinking we have to accomplish it in our own power.

4. We finally yield to God's plan (vs. 38): "Mary responded, 'I am the Lord's servant. May everything you have said about me come true.' And then the angel left her." This yielding may happen in a short time, as with Mary or Saul on the road to Damascus (Acts 9), or our doubts and fears may delay it, as with Gideon (Judg 6) or Moses (Exod 3). Eventually, though, we need to agree with God's promises.

5. We receive verification (vss. 42–45):

> Elizabeth gave a glad cry and exclaimed to Mary, "God has blessed you above all women, and your child is blessed. Why am I so honored, that the mother of my Lord should visit me? When I heard your greeting, the baby in my womb jumped for joy. You are blessed because you believed that the Lord would do what he said."

The entire plan isn't fulfilled, but either we receive confirmation from someone else, or we see the beginning of the plan being fulfilled, or both. Either way, God encourages us to move forward.

6. We glorify God (vss. 46–55): Without including the entire passage, we know this as the Magnificat, Mary's song, sung by a teenager who took God at his word. This is the whole point of promises—to glorify God through our praise and thanksgiving for what he has done and will do through us.[1]

That last step is the key to hearing God in the future. If we accept revelation and do not respond with thankfulness and praise, it's unlikely God will seek us out the next time because he knows

---

1. Harvestime, *Knowing God's Voice*, 134–37.

he will not receive glory through our lives. But if we'll glorify him and testify to his promises, he will continue to reveal himself to us throughout our lives.

We have a counterexample to Mary's more inspired response to God's promise, and that is the reaction of Zechariah, future father of John the Baptist, when the angel appeared to him. I encourage the teacher candidates I instruct to use both examples and counterexamples in their teaching, because whereas examples give us a well-marked road to follow, counterexamples warn us away from the ditches on either side (and we humans identify more with errors in practice than perfection anyway). The gospels interweave the faith and faithfulness of women such as Mary in such a way that we can hardly miss how precious the heart of a woman is to God. In the same way, but to different effect, the fear, doubt, and faithlessness of men also stand out to us in the gospels, sounding the alarm about those attitudes and actions that can hinder the outworking of the Kingdom of heaven in our lives.

The contrast presented to us in Luke chapter 1 could not be more stark: the old Zechariah, the young Mary; the priest Zechariah, the everywoman Mary; the Judean Zechariah, the Galilean Mary. Both encountered the archangel Gabriel, both initially feared the angel, both were told not to be afraid, and both were presented with a promise of the impossible. The impossibility for Zechariah had to do with his age; while the impossibility for Mary concerned her virginity. Up to that point, their experiences with their individual promises were identical. It's what happened next that distinguished them as an example and a counterexample of our potential responses to God's promises.

Both reply with a question for the messenger from God that points toward the impossibility of the promise, but with a subtle difference between the two responses:

Mary asked the angel, "But how can this happen? I am a virgin." (Luke 1:34); whereas, Zechariah said to the angel, "How can I be sure this will happen? I'm an old man now, and my wife is also well along in years." (Luke 1:18)

Responding to God's Voice

Did you catch the difference between the two questions? Wonder bubbles up from Mary's question, like, "Wow God, the deck seems stacked against you—I'd love to hear the plan!" But Zechariah wants to be "sure." His question betrays his doubts, almost demanding some kind of sign beyond the amazing vision he was receiving at that very moment. He was a priest and God was his business. Zechariah knew well that when the angel promised, "He will be a man with the spirit and power of Elijah. He will prepare the people for the coming of the Lord. He will turn the hearts of the fathers to their children, and he will cause those who are rebellious to accept the wisdom of the godly" (Luke 1:17), that Gabriel essentially was quoting from the end of the Book of Malachi. This is monumental stuff. So, as a student of Holy Scripture, implicit in Zechariah's question was the somewhat skeptical comment, "Let's break this promise down and inspect it."

Now, the mere act of questioning a promise from God is natural, almost like asking, "Did I hear you correctly, Lord?" I've asked this question many times in my life, just as you probably have. Our questions don't bother God, as long as there is at least a mustard seed of faith behind them. This was the case with Mary's question, and as a result she received a response from the angel that was incredibly personal, gentle, and reassuring:

> The angel replied, "The Holy Spirit will come upon you, and the power of the Most High will overshadow you. So the baby to be born will be holy, and he will be called the Son of God. What's more, your relative Elizabeth has become pregnant in her old age! People used to say she was barren, but she has conceived a son and is now in her sixth month. For the word of God will never fail." (Luke 1: 35-37)

But Gabriel's reaction to Zechariah's question was swift and severe:

> Then the angel said, "I am Gabriel! I stand in the very presence of God. It was he who sent me to bring you this good news! But now, since you didn't believe what I said, you will be silent and unable to speak until the child

is born. For my words will certainly be fulfilled at the proper time." (Luke 1:19–20)

Was the problem with Zechariah's question only his doubt? Or his demand for an explanation? No, the bottom line issue was the delay his question caused in bringing glory to God. I can't emphasize this enough. The promises of God, as wonderful and hopeful as they may be, aren't directed toward us at all, though we certainly benefit from them. They're intended for God, not simply as a way of bringing his plan to fruition, but to receive our worship. That is the purpose not only of promises but also of relationship, service, obedience, and living a life worthy of our calling. It's not about us; it's never been about us. God reveals our purpose in the Book of Isaiah:

> Wild animals will say 'Thank you!'
>   —the coyotes and the buzzards—
> Because I provided water in the desert,
>   rivers through the sun-baked earth,
> Drinking water for the people I chose,
>   the people I made especially for myself,
>   a people custom-made to praise me.
> (Isa 43:20–21, The Message)

The promises to Mary and to Zechariah were both fulfilled; the difference was the timing of when God received the glory. Mary's initial response was complete surrender to God's will, saying, "'I am the Lord's servant. May everything you have said about me come true'" (Luke 1:38). She followed this up in short order with the Magnificat (Luke 1:46–55), her response to the worship-words of Zechariah's wife Elizabeth, and the Magnificat has gone down in history as one of the greatest songs of praise ever uttered. Throughout, Mary kept her eyes on the prize: not on her unborn son, but on God.

Zechariah wouldn't be able to respond in worship until months after his encounter with the archangel. That's because he was struck dumb for his question, "How can I be sure this will happen?" Does this seem harsh? Not if we understand the premium

Responding to God's Voice

God places on our worship. It's everything to God, and we're privileged to praise, a right solely due to his grace.

Many years ago I had the crazy idea of getting a seminary degree, and so I took an introductory course in church history. The course taught me well—seminary wasn't for me—but it also gave me a life lesson in the form of a seminar presented by a man whose name I've now forgotten. The room was full of pastors and pastors-to-be plus me, a professor, honored to be in their midst. As the seminar wound down, the speaker made a remarkable statement to that room full of God's servants. He began, "God doesn't need you . . ." All the air went out of the room as the pastors looked around in disbelief. Then he went on, ". . . but God is very fond of you." And that, my friend, is why God gives us promises, why promises are fulfilled in our lives, why we're called to maturity, and why we have not only the right but the responsibility to return worship for blessing. God is fond of us, loves us, and wants intimate contact with us.

And even if praise is slow to come to our lips, as with Zechariah, we need to let it come. Once John the Baptist was born, Zechariah confirmed the name the baby was to be given, and then his tongue was loosened and he broke out in prophetic worship to God (Luke 1:68–79). Whether instantaneous or delayed, we need to praise our God who keeps his promises and allows us to grow up.

Conclusion

I'D LIKE TO FINISH with a parable of sorts about promises and growing up. It's not spiritual, but hopefully you'll see how it applies to what you've just read. In September 1963, a young man named George flew from England to the United States to visit his sister. She lived in Benton, a small town in the cornfields of southern Illinois. His sister showed George the limited attractions of the area, including attending a concert by a local band. Upon learning that George played guitar, the band invited him to join them onstage, and as his sister recalled later, his playing blew everyone away. There was instant respect for the young man, despite the length of his hair and his funny accent. Only five months later, the town folk of Benton sat in front of their televisions watching in disbelief as George Harrison played a rocking guitar on the *The Ed Sullivan Show*, along with his bandmates The Beatles.

When we only have the promise of growing up and while we wait for that promise to be realized, we can sometimes feel anonymous in the world. By the fall of 1963, The Beatles had taken England by storm, but to that point, America had eluded them. In fact, the American music scene was almost completely unaware of their success, confirmed by George's visit to Benton. As I've tried to emphasize in this book, timing is everything in promises coming to fruition and becoming an adult. The Beatles had a promise

Conclusion

made to them. Their manager told them they would tour America, but only once they had a number one hit there.

This finally happened at the beginning of 1964, and then it was off to the races. What the twentysomething Beatles couldn't have known then was that their big break in America would require a lot of growing up, sometimes painfully so. They quickly became so popular and sought after that they couldn't simply ride in a limo, they had to be carted around in an armored car. The Beatles also discovered they couldn't just say anything they wanted to on any topic, as it occasionally resulted in protests and threats. Eventually, they had no life on the road other than hotels and performing, and they felt they were constantly in danger. Beyond simply being more successful, none of these aspects of growing up had been anticipated by the lads from Liverpool.

So, as I've written in the preceding chapters, growing up comes in both expected and unexpected forms. I've recounted promises of deliverance, marriage, calling, and career. Days of growing up included hoped-for deliverance but also unexpected redemption; expected relationship, but unexpected perseverance and resulting godliness; expected personal fulfillment but unexpected miracles; expected obedience but unexpected adventure. As with the Israelites entering the Promised Land and the disciples of Jesus in the ten days prior to Pentecost, in order to see a promise fulfilled, sometimes we need to act but sometimes to wait.

We each have a personality that fits one or the other of these modes of operation. I'm not a thrill-seeker, and so my natural approach to life is to wait and observe. For others, waiting would be torture—they prefer to take action and let the chips fall where they may. If I'd taken any kind of action other than smiling at my tormentor during German class in college, I would have ruined what God had in store for both him and me. If I'd waited to suggest to Valya that she write her story, I may never have been her co-author.

The common denominator in the anecdotes I've shared in this book is that, whether we're waiting on God's promises to be fulfilled or we have an active role to play in their realization, God rarely gives us a free pass. Sometimes the thing that is natural for us is the most difficult. I was willing to wait to see deliverance and redemption when being bullied by Ashley, but I also had to hold my tongue, which was hard. Further, delays and discouragements, such as those I faced to win the woman God promised me, are sometimes signs we're on the right path, rather than an indication we should give up.

You might have heard the phrase, "Birth of a vision, death of a vision, birth of a vision." Often, this is how it goes with promises. God gives us a promise, the promise seems to die an untimely death, and then suddenly it springs back to life but in a different form. Why? Because we humans are prone to mess with God's promises. When we first encounter them, we react, "Who? Me? No way!" and write them off. Then after a while we may talk ourselves into it, thinking, "Why not me? I'm worth it!" And then the worst thing happens: We believe God owes us the fulfillment of the promise, and if that isn't happening the way we imagine it should, we take matters into our own hands. That's when the dream dies.

In God's good timing, and by his grace, sometimes that promise will come back to life, but only once we give it back to God and admit it was his all along. God wants to be sure we know the promise is from him, and that he will fulfill it, not us. He also wants us to know that the ultimate outcome of the promise is for his glory, not ours. In the process, we secure the wonderful benefit of growing up and being able to "adult" just fine, both spiritually and emotionally.

As in the story I told earlier of the seminary speaker and the pastors, God is very fond of us. For some inexplicable reason, he wants us on his team, and so he gives us promises to hold on to through the storms of life. Isn't that kind of God? But again, it's not about us. The intent is for us to grow and mature into the kinds of dependable disciples who have faith that God's Kingdom is coming and, in fact, is already present in us. The world doesn't need another slogan, another placard, or another cause. We need a different Kingdom, a different King, Someone who won't fail us or forsake us. We need Jesus, the source and fulfillment of our promises, the reason we can adult, every day. I'm so ready to grow up. How about you?

Bibliography

Allender, Dan B. & Longman, Tremper. *The Cry of the Soul: How Our Emotions Reveal Our Deepest Questions About God*. Colorado Springs, CO: Navpress, 2015.

Backman, Fredrik. *Anxious People*. New York: Atria, 2020.

Bakker, Jim. *The Refuge: A Look Into the Future and the Power of Living in a Christian Community*. Nashville, TN: Thomas Nelson, 2000.

Duckworth, Angela. *Grit: The Power of Passion and Perseverance*. New York: Scribner, 2018.

Enns, Peter. *How the Bible Actually Works*. New York: HarperCollins, 2020.

Evans, Rachel Held. *Inspired: Slaying Giants, Walking on Water, and Loving the Bible Again*. Nashville, TN: Thomas Nelson, 2018.

Fitzmaurice, Rosie. "This Is The Exact Age When You're Most Likely To Experience a Quarter-Life Crisis—And How To Deal With It If You Do." *Business Insider* (November 15, 2017). https://www.businessinsider.com/how-to-deal-with-a-quarter-life-crisis-2017-11

Grenchuk, Valentina & Shotsberger, Paul. *My Father Loves Me*. Kyiv, Ukraine: Institute for the Development of Christian Leadership, 2005.

Harvestime International. *Knowing God's Voice*. Harvestime International, 2000.

Noddings, Nel. *Philosophy of Education* (2nd edition). Boulder, CO: Westview, 2006.

Magee, John Gillespie, Jr. "High Flight." National Poetry Day, 1941. https://nationalpoetryday.co.uk/poem/high-flight/

Palmer, Parker J. *Let Your Life Speak: Listening for the Voice of Vocation*. San Francisco, CA: Jossey-Bass, 2000.

Parker, Kim & Igielnik, Ruth. *On the Cusp of Adulthood and Facing an Uncertain Future: What We Know About Gen Z So Far*. Pew Research Center, May 14, 2020. https://www.pewresearch.org/social-trends/2020/05/14/on-the-cusp-of-adulthood-and-facing-an-uncertain-future-what-we-know-about-gen-z-so-far-2/

Bibliography

Robinson, Dick. *More Than We Can Imagine: A Practical Guide to the Holy Spirit.* Xulon, 2013.
Sasse, Ben. *The Vanishing American Adult: Our Coming-of-Age Crisis—and How to Rebuild a Culture of Self-Reliance.* New York: St. Martin's, 2017.
Shotsberger, Paul. *Choices: God's and Ours.* Eugene, OR: Wipf and Stock, 2018.
———. *Moments that Matter.* Central, SC: Freedom's Hill, 2020.

www.ingramcontent.com/pod-product-compliance
Lightning Source LLC
Chambersburg PA
CBHW070311100426
42743CB00011B/2433